Oh, by the Way

By
Bunny Blu

PUBLISH AMERICA

PublishAmerica
Baltimore

First printing

PublishAmerica has allowed this work to remain exactly as the author intended, verbatim, without editorial input.

ISBN: 1-60610-776-3 (softcover)
ISBN: 978-1-4489-1064-9 (hardcover)
PUBLISHED BY PUBLISHAMERICA, LLLP
www.publishamerica.com
Baltimore

Printed in the United States of America

Oh, by the Way

Dedication

This book is dedicated to my husband. He has always encouraged me in all of my endeavors, without his understanding, and love this book couldn't have been written.

Acknowledgments

I wish to acknowledge my family and friends who helped me during my times of need. I can never express the gratitude to my family for all they have done for me. I thank my church for your prayers and support. Special thanks to my two dear friends who challenged me to put my thoughts on paper, you know who you are.

CHAPTER ONE

As the bright yellow Mustang took the exit ramp a little too fast, she could feel her body tense up as her fingers dig into the armrest. Not being able to see the speedometer from the passenger seat she just glanced at him. Without a verbal warning, she could feel the car begin to slow as it snaked down the pavement onto the highway.

A playful grin danced across his handsome face as he turned to look into her eyes, "What?" he asked.

A stern but simple reply, "You know I can revoke your driving privileges!" But, she couldn't maintain the pretence of anger, and they both laughed.

He reached across the black, leather console for her hand to wrap it snuggly in his own. He always made her happy just being near him. Her heart was overflowing with love, life was good for them, and they were deliriously happy. Things were calm for the moment with no huge problems hanging overhead.

Her mind wandered as she stared out the window at the bare fields, and farmhouses in the distance. It was just a few weeks ago that he had suggested they look into purchasing a newer car for her. The idea seemed to come out of thin air, but he was able to talk her into it without too much trouble.

They had purchased a new Jeep in 1999. It was her vehicle from the start. With some age on it now, the miles were beginning to add up. Although it had always been dependable, he wanted her to have a newer vehicle to drive with less mileage. He would drive a decrepit rust bucket himself, but he insisted that she have a dependable vehicle at her disposal. The thought of her being stranded on the road was intolerable. He did not want even the slightest possibility of a breakdown leaving her stranded on the roadside. If he had mechanical problems with his ride, he could usually get things going again, at least long enough to run it back to his workshop. All she could do was look under the hood, and say, "Well, the engine is still there."

At her insistence they had purchased a used truck for him last winter to replace the ancient one he drove. The old, blue Chevy was beginning to nickel and dime them to death. It seemed that every weekend he was replacing something on it. Logic told them it was time to sell it while they had it running. They needed something that would be easier to maintain.

After several months of searching, they had found a newer truck to replace it. It was clean, with a new paint job, and surprisingly enough in their price range. What a bargain they thought they had found only to discover it had a few problems they would have to deal with very soon.

That money pit had costs them a bundle. They knew when they made the purchase that the tires needed to be replaced. New ones were installed within the first week. He didn't need to add the frustration, or danger of a flat tire at highway speeds to add to the stress of his daily commute.

The transmission went within the first month. If he only had the time to do the repairs himself, he could have saved them a lot. Neither one of them could afford to miss work by having a vehicle down, so they had to shell out the cash to have the job professionally done. It had cost them quite a bit to repair, but they didn't have the luxury of time to spend working on it in what little spare time he had.

Brakes were the next to go. JW and Bunny installed new, rear brakes themselves in his workshop at home one weekend to avoid another costly visit to the mechanic. He had done all the dirty work. She just handed him tools, and ducked when the occasional wrench was flung aside in frustration. With both of them covered in dirt and grease, she was finally able to make him laugh at the situation. Together, playfully, they finished the job.

All that was just to keep it road worthy and going, but they had managed to keep it going so far. He had put a lot of miles on that truck since then in the past year. His daily drive was 1 ½ hours each morning to get to work, the same for the return trip home. A total of 3 hours on the highway each day took a toll on both the truck and the driver. Every time he turned the key, she prayed that it held together for another trip. After the initial costly repairs it had run well for him though.

After all of the constant highway abuse they had made the decision to look into buying a newer car for her, the truck would retire, so to speak. They would use it only for hauling and towing the "farm" trailer. He would get the hand-me-down Jeep, she would get the newly purchased car for her daily drive. It sounded like the logical solution to the problem they faced. The search began for one that would be suitable for their needs. A quest was on for a car, one that would be practical and cost efficient to operate. Every weekend they both began to scan the newspaper ads for a car. It was a task neither of them enjoyed, but it was a necessary task.

She'd lost her heart to a bright, red, 1965 Mustang her father had repaired in the shop that he owned when she was in high school. Her brothers had taken their turn in the shop helping in the family business before her. They had both married and moved on to other careers. Now, she had become his hired help. Some of the men he hired worked a few short weeks, then never showed up again. The faithful employees on staff could not handle the extra workload created when that occurred. Somebody had to help get the cars out on time, so she had pitched in after school and on weekends. This insured that the cars were always ready for the customers when promised.

She had turned out to be as skillful as her brothers. Her father was able to quickly teach her how to sand primer and prep cars for painting. Giving them a final cleaning and polish job soon fell into her capable hands. Quickly, Bunny had been accepted as one of the team. She had worked by her father's side daily in his shop, sometimes until 10 or 11 in the evening.

When she wasn't helping him in the shop she took over bookkeeping duties with her mother in the office. Since his shop was located just behind their home it was hard to work normal hours, someone was always dropping off, or picking up a vehicle. Tow trucks often delivered cars in need of repair work at all hours of the day and night. Her father taught her the value of honesty, hard work, and flexibility.

Extra care had gone into her work on that Mustang before it was turned over to the owner. It was polished and shined to perfection with her calloused hands. She was thrilled when her father had given her permission to back it out of the garage into the nearby parking area. Her imagination ran wild as she dreamed of driving it on the open road. She could almost feel the wind in her hair and hear the roar of the engine as it raced down the highway.

That was years ago, the thought of owning anything like that had long ago been erased from her mind. There were always other things that took priority over something frivolous like that. Never in a million years had she dreamed of ever having a Mustang of her own, but the love of her life was seriously talking about making her dream come true. He had found several Mustangs listed in a newspaper ad. One Saturday morning he asked her if she would like to finally, once in their life, just go nuts. They would buy something for fun, not practicality. He spoiled her way too much, and she loved it!

After looking at several dealerships, her eye was caught not by a red one but a bright yellow...Screaming Yellow according to the tag in the window of the 2005 Mustang. It was used, but in December of

2005 still considered new by her standards. It was the most beautiful car she had ever seen. A black, leather interior offset the bright, yellow exterior. It was more than she had ever dreamed of having.

Her Prince, as she called him because believe me she had met her fair share of toads in life, gave her the go ahead to complete the transaction. This was a dream come true. She was going to have a Mustang of her very own.

They would not have a car payment hanging over their heads either. They had scrimped to save the money to pay for it. Her hands trembled as she wrote the check to finalize the deal. Once that was done, the prize was hers. Her Prince even arranged to have the Santa at the dealership hand her the keys to "Her Pony." Photos were taken to document that it was a gift from Santa…Her Santa.

Today they were taking it out on their first real road trip. They were going to his company dinner. Everyone would get to see the beautiful gift she had been given for Christmas. All of his co-workers had heard about it. He had even shown them pictures of Santa giving her the keys to her new car. Now they could see it up close and personal. They could tell just how generous this man of hers was, and how shamefully he spoiled her.

The silent reflection was broken by a question, "What are you thinking about, Bunny?"

She was startled back to the present. Her gaze was now fixed on the man in the driver's seat. His piercing, blue eyes made her heart skip a beat. He was so dashing sitting there in his uniform. Displayed on one shoulder was the American flag, the other one held his unit patch. His last name was above his right breast pocket, and the words U. S. Army rested over his heart. The set of crossed pistols to indicate Military Police were worn proudly on the uniform, as well as his hard earned Captain's bars.

"Oh, just thinking about how happy I am, and how fortune I am to be your wife," was her honest, heart felt reply.

She sighed softly squeezing his hand. He gave her a gentle squeeze back sliding his hand from hers. His expression changed from a playful mood to take on a more serious tone. His hands were now positioned on the steering wheel at ten and two, his jaw muscle had tightened slightly.

He looked straight ahead trying to make his statement sound ever so casual, "Oh, by the way, you may hear talk of Iraq today."

Ok, not a problem. Iraq had been in the news for years now. No big deal.

His eyes darted in her direction looking for a response before continuing, "Well, you see they are going to be talking about us as a unit leaving to go there."

No reaction from the blonde in the seat next to him. Her focus was now intently aimed at him, and every word he spoke.

He continued while he had her full attention, "I'll have to go to Iraq for awhile...um...like for a year."

It felt like someone had hit her in the face with a bucket of ice water. What had he just said...Iraq...leaving me for a year? It wasn't possible!

What had just happened? Her happy, little world had crumbled at that last sentence. No, this wasn't happening, not to her. She folded her hands neatly in her lap fighting to find words, some words, any words. Don't panic, now is not the time to let him see her panic. Calm, she must remain calm. Dear God, help her find something to say without screaming. Oh, how she wanted to scream.

"Bunny, did you hear me? I have to go to Iraq," he pleaded for some kind of reaction.

Ok, I can do this she assured herself. Taking in a quick breath she was finally able to say, "Just how long have you known about this?"

A sheepish answer, "Oh, awhile now," was all she heard.

How could he have kept this a secret from her? They always told each other everything. They had no secrets. That was the success to their marriage. No secrets, ever.

Why hadn't she seen this coming? Is that why he had so much

training going on lately? Hadn't she been paying attention? How could she have missed this coming? So many questions were racing through her mind. Nothing was making any sense. Her brain was apparently going through a short circuit, information just wasn't being processed.

"Say something," he pleaded.

"I really don't know what to say. When were you planning on telling me about this little trip?" she implored.

"Well, since we are about 20 minutes away from the Armory, and everybody else knows about this I thought I'd better speak up now. I didn't want you to hear it from someone else," was his answer.

She sat in shock still reeling from the blow that her life had just taken. Only twenty minutes to get it together before she faced the rest of the troops, and their families to attend the annual Christmas dinner for the unit. Great. Really great! She wanted to crawl under her seat. She wanted to hide, to run, to avoid this collision with the statement he had just thrown at her.

Once again he broke the fragile silence, "It will be okay, really. I love you. The reason I didn't tell you earlier that I had to go was because I didn't want you to worry any longer than necessary."

"So, was my car a bribe to help soften the blow?" she asked.

"Kind of...in a way. I didn't want to worry about you dealing with car repairs while I was gone. Besides, I needed something going for me when I broke the news to you," he finally confessed.

She tried to see things from his point of view. She would have worried as soon as he told her of the upcoming mission, telling her earlier wouldn't have lessened the impact. She had a way of obsessing about situations, even those she knew she had no control over. He had always put her first in everything he did in life. Her anger began to melt away as she thought of the agony he must have gone through keeping this secret from her. In her heart, she knew he would never hurt her intentionally.

She reached out to touch his cheek softly with her fingertips as a single tear trickled down her own. Her bitterness ebbed away as she gave him a faint smile, "It's ok. We've gone through a lot. We'll get through this."

"Thank God! I thought you'd kill me, or leave me, or something," relief pouring through him. His jaw muscle relaxed, and he managed to give her a smile in return. "I'm sorry, so sorry to do this to us."

Her mind returned to the past, thinking back in time she remembered the hard times they'd come through. But, she had meant every word of those vows she'd taken years ago. She had spoken them clearly, "to honor and to cherish, in sickness and in health, for better and for worse, for richer and for poorer." Well, they'd certainly seen it all. She'd taken that oath twice, once before a judge at the courthouse, again when he held a surprise, official church wedding for her.

He had been working in a large town almost four hours from their home in the country, which meant spending the entire workweek away from home. Living out of a dark, basement apartment furnished with one chair, a twin bed, old card table, a small TV, and microwave oven. He would leave long before sunup on Monday mornings. Every evening he would call home to make sure she was safely tucked in, just to tell her how much he loved her.

After his shift ended on Friday evenings, he faced the big city traffic to fight his way home to be able to spend two days with her. Most of the weekend was spent on yard work and household repairs. It made her heart ache to think of him alone in that place. but he told her that he had to pay his dues. A transfer would not bring him home for 18 months. During that entire time, he lived out of a suitcase to provide a better life for them.

It was during this separation that he saved the meager allowance he was allotted for lunch and spending money for her real church wedding. On their tenth wedding anniversary, he surprised her in the little chapel with stained, glass windows. After the Sunday service, he bent down on one knee to ask her to be his bride, again, in front of everyone. Through a cascade of tears, she said, "Yes." That day they renewed their wedding vows before friends and family.

He used most of his allowance to send back home. With some help from a relative, he planned the entire thing: invitations, flowers, a real wedding cake, and punch. He was truly the love of her life, her very own real, life Prince. There was no question that they adored each other.

"Listen, if you think you can get rid of me that easy you are quite mistaken," she was finally able to proclaim with all the love in her heart. With that statement a stronger bond was forged between them. He was reassured of this woman's love for him. She knew she had chosen her husband well. No other man could hold a candle to him. He was unmistakably the most loving man she had ever met.

The rest of the drive continued with him trying to explain the way things would happen. Not a lot of details just yet, no timetables, and no dates on when they would leave, just the fact that they would be going. That was enough for now. She didn't want to know any more, she already knew too much. She tried to be positive, and upbeat, giving a nod here, or a word of encouragement there. Twenty minutes seemed like an eternity and yet not long enough.

The Mustang turned into the lot behind the Armory to find the Captain's parking spot. It was show time; she had to pull off the biggest acting job of a lifetime now. He jumped out of the driver's seat to pull open her door, forever the gentleman. Just how many more times would he be able to do that before they called him away? She bit her lip, forced a smile, and took his arm. She was proud to be the wife of a Soldier, this Soldier, her Soldier.

The rest of the day was a blur of activities. She followed her husband aimlessly. She was introduced to other Soldier's families; wives, husbands, mothers, fathers, sons, and daughters. Some of them seemed to be in the same state of mind as she was. Utter confusion summed it up best at this point in time. Well, at least that helped her knowing she wasn't alone. Misery loves company.

She found herself shuffling through a "chow line" for the full

Christmas fare. Although the surroundings were festive, she was not. There were all her favorites, but she felt sure that she wouldn't be able to eat a bite. She requested a half portion on everything, hoping he wouldn't notice if the plate went untouched.

She was seated next to a bubbly brunette, a Sergeant's wife. Both husbands ran off to attend to military matters leaving the two alone to finish their meal. She didn't realize the important role Tracey would play in her life in the months to come. It was not by chance they were thrown together that day, from that meeting a friendship would blossom. They would find comfort, and support from the bond of friendship they would come to share.

Both made small talk, pushing the food around on their plates, nervously taking bites of the tidbits. Door prizes were handed out while children were called up to receive gifts from Santa. The youngster's squeals of delight filled the room as they tore through the paper, and bows to reveal the treasures each box held for them.

Then, finally it was over, and farewells were spoken. He ushered her to the waiting car for the trip home. She sank into the seat glad to have the ordeal over. The day hadn't turned out to be the one she had hoped for by any means. Instead of a day of carefree fun, it had turned into her worst nightmare.

The drive home was agonizingly long. Her head was pounding with every heartbeat, making her feel as limp as a rag doll, totally drained. The various emotions that ran through her mind throughout the day had taken a devastating toll. All she wanted to do was to make it home to rid herself of the red, Christmas dress and shoes. Curling up in the warmth, and safety of JW's strong arms, she could finally let the tears flow that had been held at bay all day.

She tried desperately to carry on a normal conversation for the next hour and half, letting him do much of the talking. She attempted to steer the conversation away from the news he had broken to her earlier in the day. She preferred to talk about the decorations, the cute children, the people she had met that day, anything other than the fact that he was leaving her. But, her mind raced on with the announcement of the deployment as they called it, whatever THEY called it, that's all she could think about.

Once in the security of his embrace, the tears did come, they came in uncontrollable sobs. He let her cry trying to comfort her by gently stroking her shoulder length, honey blonde hair, whispering words of comfort to her. Exhaustion finally overcame her as she slipped into a worried slumber wrapped in his arms.

They decided to not break the news to anyone until after the holidays. Christmas was going to be celebrated without the news of him leaving for Iraq hanging over the joyful season. Christmas Eve was spent with friends at the huge annual potluck. Family gathered for a feast on Christmas Day. Presents were exchanged, and for a time Bunny was able to push the intrusion of the deployment from her mind. She was going to celebrate the season with him. They were going to enjoy being together with the people they loved.

They stayed at home to ring in the New Year, just the two of them as they had done for as long as she could remember. For the past several years JW had cooked and served her supper to celebrate New Year's Eve. He prepared her favorite shrimp scampi along with a baked potato, and salad. This year he had splurged adding a steak to the fare. He proceeded to produce a box of her favorite chocolates he had hidden away for her indulgence. It was a much needed quiet celebration after the excitement of shopping and celebrating Christmas.

During the following weeks, JW and Bunny began talking about the plans they would have to make before his departure. JW and Bunny had bought a 6acre tract in the spring of 1993. He made it his mission to have a beautiful house built for Bunny. Plans had been drawn up, and her home began to take shape. Weather conditions caused delays in the construction. They soon found themselves homeless when they sold the home they occupied before their home was finished.

It was Bunny's parents that came to the rescue. They parked their camper in the front yard for them to live in. Dad stored all of their belongings in the garage that was once used as his business property. Rainfall during that spring and summer was extremely heavy. The yard turned into a muddy mess. It was a trial for them and their son during the next several months.

The rivers throughout the state overflowed their banks flooding farm fields, and swallowing up entire towns. National Guard units were activated to patrol flooded areas. JW's unit was called to help out with massive flooding in the western part of the state. He wasn't there during most of the construction stage, leaving Bunny and Mick to undertake the final details. After five weeks JW returned to inspect the almost finished project. Six months after beginning the process they were able to move into their home.

A chicken coop with an attached outdoor pen was built the following year for Bunny. Several years later a workshop was added to the property near the house with a fence between them to create a courtyard, filled with fragrant flowers and shrubs. It provided a peaceful retreat they needed to lounge in after their hectic workweek.

A painful decision to sell their home was made shortly after Bunny had been made aware of the deployment. Her beautiful house was on the market. They had listed it with a local realtor to move closer to his job, so he didn't have three hours of "windshield time" every day, as JW called it. It would be easier on both of them the closer they got to the deployment date. He wanted to make it easier on Bunny by moving her into a smaller home with less ground to care for in his absence. The family support group would be near if she needed assistance, too.

They seriously started looking at homes in, and around the town where he worked. They would be ready to make the jump to a new home when theirs finally sold. If they couldn't sell to settle into a home at least a month before he left they'd stay put. She would have to adjust to whatever took place.

She did not want the responsibility of selling one home while buying another without him. He didn't want her to have to carry that burden without his help. Just the transaction alone would be a monumental feat with him thousands of miles from home. Moving everything from one home to another would be much more than she could handle. There would be enough changes in both their lives in the coming year. A different home would only add stress neither of them needed at this time. If they stayed in their present home, it would be her responsibility to maintain for an entire year. Added to that task was the up-keep for the two tractors, the truck, Jeep, and recently purchased Mustang.

She knew she could manage to care for her chickens. She had a small flock of just eight at the time. She raised chicks that laid eggs with blue and green eggshells, so everyday she gathered the eggs was like going on an Easter egg hunt. Her basket was always filled with brightly colored eggs. She amazed overnight guests with her "green eggs" and ham breakfasts.

The sound of her hens clucking softly at her feet as she went about her chores was well worth the effort of their care. It was just one of the small things in life that made her happy. The fresh eggs and occasional chicken dinner were just an added bonus. She had grown up having chickens, ducks, and little pigs. When she had the chance it seemed only natural for her to have a few critters here, too.

They had raised pigs in the past, but they both knew she couldn't handle their care without his help. A little 40 lb. piglet was one thing to care for, a market weight 250 lb. hog was a lot to keep under control. Fences had to be constantly monitored, or they would burrow out to run off through the yard. Hauling in feed and water would be a monumental task for her alone.

Last fall's hogs were gone. All of them ended up in someone's freezer, or were sold to a local market. Every pen, hut, and feeder had to be sold. They were officially going out of the hog farming business. It had proved to be a hobby anyway, and not a money making venture.

What farm would be complete without the faithful watchdog? She was totally devoted to Bunny. Many months of training went into making her pup have manners. She needed to have a dog that would obey. Goldie soon learned that her master wanted obedience. Commands were repeated until the little dog yielded to Bunny's will. When she complied with a command, a generous reward of doggie treats and praise followed. It hadn't taken Bunny long to mold her into a wonderful companion. Occupying an outdoor kennel, she maintained a watch over the property for any intruders.

Bunny also had an indoor cat for company. Larkin had been adopted from a local animal shelter. In reality, it was the kitten that chose them for adoption. Her white fur with just a touch of yellow on the tips, and her little, pink nose had them from the first "meow." Of course, cats can never be trained to obey. The old adage that cats had staff, not owners certainly applied in this case.

Bunny was doubtful at first that she could keep everything going by herself. JW was always there to take care of things for her. He handled all the heavy lifting and most of the yard work. She wasn't allowed to lift over 20 lbs. due to back problems, and multiple operations to repair them. That was JW's main concern, also. Somehow they would have to make things come together for her if they didn't move. She couldn't afford to injure her back again. Her doctor warned her that a third major operation might not be an option. No matter what happened they had to find a way to make things work for her.

"I got the time frame for our departure. Sometime in the fall," he said as he slumped into his favorite spot on the sofa after coming in from his long drive home.

As he unlaced his combat boots, she realized the clock was running faster than she had expected it to. January was almost gone. No way was she ready for him to be leaving in the fall, the fall, ok, was that September, October, or maybe November?

"They are going to have meetings to help families prepare for all of this soon. You should go. Maybe meet some of the other wives, get to know them. That way you'll have people to hang out with while I'm gone," he added.

She simply nodded, and went into the kitchen to finish supper. Fighting back the tears welling up in her dark green eyes she felt the dread of sending him away return to weigh on her heart once again. Concentrate on now, right now. He is here now, live in the moment. Tomorrow will take care of itself. Please, God, let me handle this, give me the strength for today was her plea. By the time he had taken a quick shower and changed into faded jeans with a well-worn flannel shirt, she managed to greet him in the kitchen with a warm hug.

"I love you so much, so very much," she murmured as she slipped her arms around his neck. She gave him a quick peck on the check before pulling away from his embrace.

She served up plates of steaming, hot pasta, and garlic bread to go with the bright, green salads already on the table. They chattered through supper to begin planning what they would need to do in the near future. For now he was here, and he belonged to her.

JW had a meeting after work at the Armory one evening, which gave Bunny time to seek out help. After dealing with the bottled up pain for weeks, she needed to release her frustration and get a handle on her confusion.

She needed to see her friend Beatrice. Their friendship began when Bea and Slick moved in across the street from Bunny years ago. Bunny had waddled her 8½month pregnant body down her sloping front yard to invite them over to share supper with her family. It was indeed a feast; grilled hotdogs, potato salad, and baked beans were all she had to offer, but, they had accepted the meal along with the friendship.

Bea and Bunny had weathered many of the storms of life together since then. They were true friends. The kind of friends that stay with you through every problem large or small no matter what happened to come your way. To admit how long they had known each other would allow everyone to know their real age, and they both refused to do that.

Bea was a couple years younger than Bunny but very wise indeed. Bunny valued her wisdom, and ability to see things logically. She had never failed to stand by her side during any crisis. She needed wisdom and logic, now more than ever. She needed the comfort of a dear friend. Her fingers fumbled as she punched the numbers into the phone. She waited for the familiar voice to pick up.

"Hello," it was Bea. Bunny almost lost if then.

"Hey, what ya doing?" Bunny's voice almost cracked.

"Nothing. What do you need?" Bea replied.

"I just need to talk if you have the time," Bunny hoped she hadn't sounded too needy.

Bea knew her friend too well, "What's wrong?" she asked.

"I'll tell you when I get there. Can I come over?" Bunny said almost pleading now.

"Sure, Slick is gone, and Jean is out. It'll just be just the two of us," Bea had cleared the way for her.

"Thanks, I'll be in shortly," was Bunny's response.

She was thankful that Bea's husband, Slick, was practicing with his band that played gigs on the weekends. Their daughter was probably attending one of her college classes. JW would be late getting home himself. The walls were closing in on her. She had to escape before she suffocated. She had to see her best friend face to face, a simple phone call would not suffice.

Bea lived in a town 7 miles east of Bunny. The Mustang roared down the slushy roadway to her home in record time. Bea was waiting to welcome her at the door. She dropped her boots on the mat inside the door, and threw her coat over a chair. Bea poured both of them a Diet Coke.

Bea turned to her friend, "Okay, girl give it up."

Bunny blurted out, "JW got the word that he's going to be going to Iraq," before she lost control, and started to cry.

"When?" Bea asked in shock at the sudden announcement.

"This fall he's leaving for a year. I'll be all alone," Bunny sobbed.

Bea's loving nature took over. She held Bunny letting her cry, adding tears of her own. Bea hurt when her friends hurt. They were sharing the pain together just as they had in all of their years of friendship. When one hurt the other felt the pain. Pain that was shared between them was easier to bear, together they would bare the burden of JW marching off to war.

After Bunny had no more tears to give up, Bea pushed her an arm's length away. With a hand positioned on each one of Bunny's shoulders, she looked her square in the eye to state firmly, "We will get through this. I will be there for you. You have always been there for me. We will do this together. Whatever you need, whenever you need it, you've got it."

"Bea, you are a true friend. I knew I could count on you," Bunny held onto the pledge her friend had just spoken with conviction.

That's all Bunny needed to hear. She had the love and the support of her friend. They had in fact shared all of life's joys, and trials head on together, side by side, and hand in hand. That made the task to come easier to face. They continued to visit for several hours. Bunny felt renewed, and stronger when she backed the car out of the drive to head for home.

She knew that JW's departure was going to leave a large, empty hole in her life. She had begun to gather her troops for the war she must wage on the home front in JW's absence. Bea was just the first of many Bunny would recruit in her fight to keep the home fires burning. She was the beginning of Bunny's support staff. She had a feeling she would need a full platoon of mighty warriors before JW returned. A lot could happen in the time he would be gone. Battle plans had to be drawn, and provisions made to face whatever the future held for her.

CHAPTER TWO

Knowing that they had to inform their family and friends about JW's deployment, they began talking to them over the next several weeks. They had a lot of people to tell so the sooner they started the sooner it would be over. Bunny thought it would be best to begin with their son and his wife.

It had been just over six years since Mick and Leann had married. They had recently informed Bunny and JW that were expecting their first child. That could mean that JW may miss the baby's birth. He would certainly miss much of the first year of his grandchild's life if he did managed to be there for the blessed event. It tore at Bunny's heart to inform the young couple of his departure.

They were the first on the list. It was very difficult on everyone. Mick and Leann vowed they would help out while JW was gone. Both were reliable, and JW knew he could entrust them to care for Bunny. He loved them so. It was breaking his heart to leave them.

Since that encounter was so emotionally draining, JW and Bunny decided to take it slow in telling the rest of the family. No sense in everyone starting to worry ahead of time, but sooner or later everyone had to be told because his absence for a year was going to be noticed. After all, she could not just go around telling them he was in the shower every time some one wanted to talk to him.

Bunny knew it was going to be hard for his parents. JW and his brother belonged to the same unit, which meant both would be leaving. His mother would have to carry the burden of two sons leaving her to go overseas. They tried to break the news as gently as possible to them.

One by one they told all their family and friends about his leaving for Iraq, except Bunny's parents. They were going to be the hardest ones to tell. They adored JW, loving him as if he were their own son. Both of them were well past 80, mom was not in the best of health, and dad had been battling cancer for four years. It was in remission for the time being, but Bunny feared that springing this kind of news on them would cause a tragedy of some kind to occur. No way did she want that on her head.

She called one of her brothers, Chuck, to help her. Together they devised a plan. He could pop in for a visit with the folks. Bunny and JW would plan on going down the next weekend. They would carefully break the news to them. Chuck and his wife, Marge, would then be able to stay on a few days with the folks keeping an eye on things. Chuck was a retired doctor. That made her feel better knowing he would be there if anything did happened, he would know what to do. It was the perfect plot.

Much to everyone's surprise mom and dad took the news fairly well. They had a multitude of questions, but all in all it had worked out very well. Bunny and JW could mark the last names off the list.

JW was concerned about Bunny being alone. He knew she was a social creature and loved people. How was she going to survive without some activities to occupy her spare time?

"You have an entire year to do something. Why don't you take some college classes?" he asked her more than once.

"Because I don't want to go to college. I'm too old," she insisted each time he brought up the subject.

The fact was she was too scared to go to college. She was afraid she wouldn't be able to handle the stress of him being gone, classes, work, and the upkeep around the house. She wanted to be free to help Mick and Leann when the baby arrived anyway. After all, she needed to set aside plenty of time to spoil the new grandbaby. They may need her help, and she wanted to always be available for them.

"You could get your accounting degree which would help you with work," he always threw that in to back up his argument.

Her job as an office manager did include accounting. A degree would help in her current position, or help her land another one elsewhere. She felt like she just answered the phone, becoming a troubleshooter for the sales staff most of the time. She used to love her job, but it had become a chore to get up every morning to drag her weary body into the office lately. She had not been sleeping very well, the stress of the pending deployment plus all the other chaos in her life was beginning to wear her down.

"I just don't want to go. Now leave me alone," she almost screamed as she left the room.

Knowing that enrolling in any college class was a closed subject at this point, he managed to get her to join a local car club. Since she loved her car it was easy to convince her to do that. It was for Mustangs, and she could fill her social calendar with as many club meetings and events as she wished. That eased his mind a little knowing that she would at least have some interest outside of her home to keep her busy.

March rolled in all too soon. On JW's drill weekend, a support group would be holding a meeting to help the families adjust to all the confusion that had been thrown into their lives. Bunny rode with him to the Armory. She even allowed him to drive the Mustang under her close supervision.

She would have to find a way to occupy the morning since the meeting wouldn't take place until 1 that afternoon, at least they were together. She wouldn't have to drive up in a couple of hours alone, and be stuck with two cars to drive back home. They laughed at each other's jokes all the way to the Armory enjoying the pleasure of each other's company.

He sat her in his brother's office to get them both a cup of coffee. Sitting in his office reminded her that both of them were leaving loved ones to go to war. She had been able to block that from her mind since breaking the news to JW's parents. Bunny would have a husband and a brother-in-law in Iraq. She could not imagine the anguish his mother was going through knowing two of her sons would be in harm's way.

"There are fresh donuts down the hall, help yourself if you want one. Gotta go." JW told her as he scurried into the room with the coffee mugs, and sped off to a meeting.

She grabbed a donut, returning to start thumbing through the paper. She found it almost impossible to focus on any article ending up just scanning through the store flyers. The hallway had become a sea of green uniforms moving past the doorway in waves. It wasn't long until she was gathered up by several people to help set up for the meeting.

The next several hours flew by as she helped set up tables with information packets, that's where JW found her. He whisked her away for a quick lunch, so they could get back for the session. They were both starving. A couple of gyros and fries from a nearby vender were quickly devoured. She had survived the morning with her spirits intact for the most part.

When they returned for the meeting, JW had a few things to attend to, Army paper work was all he told her. He had to leave for a while but assured her he would be back before the meeting started. She wasn't ready for the avalanche of papers and forms she was given. It was a bit over whelming to say the least. Bunny spotted Tracey in the crowd. What a lifesaver, at least it was a face she knew. They found seats to wait for the return of their husbands.

JW and John filtered into the room with all the other Soldiers to find their wives giggling like little schoolgirls over a joke one of them had made. As John slipped into his chair beside his wife, he made the comment, "I think we've created a monster putting these two together."

JW just shook his head saying, "Too late, they've already bonded." That caused both women to giggle even more.

The meeting began, the room became quiet, and the giggles gave way to focus on the matters about to be addressed. Speaker after speaker told the families what to expect, paperwork they needed, how to deal with various issues, and so forth. Then the announcement was made that the unit would be heading for Iraq in September or October, but (oh Bunny hated "buts" it never failed after someone used that word something unpleasant usually followed.) But, the unit would be leaving in June for 3 months of training in the states before going overseas, then the 12 months of deployment would begin after they reached Iraq. The real clock would not begin ticking off the time until then. They called it "boots on the ground" for a year.

Bunny found tears stinging her eyes as she tried to focus on the next speaker. They just added on another 3 months. She worked as an accountant. She could do the math. That was 15 months not 12 as stated before. She had her mind set for a departure in the fall not in the middle of summer, not in June. They had things to do. Nothing was ready for him to leave then, the house wasn't ready, the vehicles weren't ready, the financial aspect of it all wasn't ready. Worst of all she wasn't ready!

She felt the heat in the room as the rosy glow drained from her face. She thought for a moment she might faint. 'Get hold of yourself girl' her mind kept repeating as she tried to focus on what was being discussed next.

JW took her by the arm. The meeting had ended. He watched her closely realizing how the update on the timeline had affected her. A weak smile traveled across her pale face as she rose to her feet. Tracey gave her a quick hug, twirling away with a hasty goodbye, both women were feeling the same insane panic. A new deadline had been issued meaning less time than they originally thought they had. She had so much to do, so much to say, and even less time to accomplish it all.

She felt better once they were outside and the cool spring air swirled around her. She could breath at least. Once again the Army had turned her world upside down and inside out. How could they do this to her? They were destroying her world bit by bit.

It was not only the Army that was destroying her world. March turned into a month of devastating thunderstorms and numerous tornadoes. For three weekends in a row their state had been pounded by the ongoing, unpredictable weather. The second group of storms brought destruction to Bunny's beloved home. They heard the warnings on TV that their home was in the path of a tornado. Before they could get Goldie inside from her kennel, and gather up Larkin to head for the shelter of the basement, the power went out. They found their way to the basement to huddle around the weather radio with flashlights to listen to the incoming updates.

It was over in a matter of minutes. After the all clear was given, they headed upstairs only to find water streaming into the living room. The wind from the storm had ripped the gray vinyl siding loose allowing water to pour into the room, running down one entire wall, and into the carpet. It took hours to mop up water while moving furniture, and family treasures to safer nooks in the house before they could go to bed. At least it was a matter the insurance company would fix. They could add that to the list of recent stressful events.

The storm damage made a decision for them about leaving their house on the market. They would have to remain in their home now. No one would put in a bid on a damaged house. Thankfully, a proposal, and pending contract they had put in to purchase another home had fallen through at the last minute a week or so before that. At least they wouldn't be stuck with two homes.

Parades of perspective buyers running through the house at all hours would stop now. Bunny hated strangers opening up her closets allowing personal items to be put on display. Much to all the realtors dislike Bunny and JW wouldn't budge on their stand to be present at every showing. They learned from the sale of their previous house that giving someone keys to your home without supervision only caused a lot of grief.

Even with the storm damage they knew that they had to step up their preparations for JW's departure. Bunny would just have to take time off work to deal with the insurance adjuster, and lining up contractors to complete the needed repairs. She would be put in charge because he may indeed be gone before repairs were completed, or even started. In the mean time, they had a ton of other things to attend to.

They began searching for items that needed to be replaced before he left. It would give JW piece of mind knowing that he had done everything he could to make this easier on Bunny. A new refrigerator was first on the list of items to purchase, this would be the first new one they would own. The previous ones were used, or handed down from family members. Both of them knew the old one in the kitchen was not far from a total break down. It was 20 years old, and had seen better days years ago. The constant noise it made when the motor kicked in reminded them of that fact.

It was suppose to be simple. The delivery driver would bring it in, hook it up, then haul the old one away. But, it proved to be much more complicated. The young man that installed it broke the water line as he hooked it up to the icemaker. There was a flood in the kitchen of Biblical proportions before the turn off valve was located, and the floodgates were closed. So, the appliance sat in the middle of the kitchen for two days as they waited on a plumber to repair the damaged line and for the walls to dry out.

JW went over the schedules he maintained on all the vehicles. He patiently showed her how to check the fluid levels on everything telling her to make sure they all got into the shop on time for regular oil changes and tire rotations. Bunny took notes to remind her of her new duties. They came to the old 1952 Ford 8N tractor that only he knew how to run. As much as he tried to instruct her on hooking up, and running the mower, she just couldn't do it.

Bunny knew he was frustrated with her, but the PTO for the mower was too heavy and difficult for her to attach to the tractor. She just wasn't strong enough to do it. Nothing was going right, she was trying her best, but it was beyond her capabilities. He kept pounding it into her head the importance of getting the PTO in place. She could barely get the tractor started, and failed to keep it running once she did.

"What part of I can't do it do you not understand?" Bunny screamed, "I am trying. I am willing, but not able to do it. Besides, it's your fault I have to learn all this crap because you are leaving me here alone. I wasn't my idea to send you half way around the world. Whatever problem we have with this piece of junk is your fault not mine!"

There, she said it. As soon as the words were out of her mouth, she wished she could take them back. It was the truth as she saw it. It hadn't been her plan to have him go away. She resented the fact that she was going to be abandoned for at least 15 months. She could see the hurt on JW's face that her words had inflicted.

He shouted back at her, "Well, it wasn't my plan either. I am a Soldier. Soldiers take orders. They go where they are told to go. I have to go. Like it or not I am leaving, so just get used to it!"

Bunny started to cry bitter tears. Why did she have to be so blunt unleashing all her anger on him? All he was trying to do was prepare her for the difficulties she would have to face in the coming months. There she was shooting arrows of resentment at him for things he had no control over, and they hit their mark. She had hurt him, unintentionally, with the words she had spoken in anger. Not anger toward him, but anger toward whoever it was that was taking him away. He happened to be the one on the receiving end of it though.

"I'm sorry. I don't know what's wrong with me," she confessed to him.

He was still hurt, but he held her to him, assuring her that they would figure something out.

"I love you. I know you are confused. I also know how strong you are. You CAN do this," he told her allowing his own anger to subside as he brushed away her tears.

His search began to buy a mower for Bunny. He agonized over buying a used one verses a new one. What if he bought a used one, then it turned out to be a lemon? There he would be thousands of miles away, while she would be back at home with a useless piece of lawn equipment. She wouldn't know how to fix it, and he wouldn't be there to help her. He did find a new John Deere tractor that would suit their needs well, but it was going to cost much more than they had allotted for that one item.

"I just don't know what to do Bunny. If I don't get the new tractor, I'll worry about you all the time. It's more than we should spend, especially now," he groaned as he poured over a stack of brochures.

"I know you physically can't handle the big tractor, she's just too much for you to take on. The little mowing tractor will never last another year if you use it to mow all this grass. It's just for trimming," he continued.

"Just do it. You have wanted to own a John Deere tractor all your life. We need a mower. Look they have a special deal going on, we won't have to pay it all now. We can get it at 0% interest, and make monthly payments," she insisted. "Besides, you are driving both of us crazy with this issue. It needs to be settled. It's either we spend the money on a new tractor for you, or another back surgery for me. You choose."

Rarely was she this adamant, and he knew it. JW took her to test drive the tractor. He wanted to make sure that she was confident in running it. The salesman was a veteran himself. He totally understood the problems involved when a wife was left to run the homestead. He had spent 12 months in Iraq in the early stages of the war.

He patiently showed her how to operate the tractor, then turned her loose in the lot. It was easy to operate and handled smoothly. It had power steering, a comfortable seat, and easy to locate controls. She could even handle changing out the hydraulic lines to drop the end loader to use the mower. The mower could stay on the tractor permanently. No lifting, and no PTO to hook up. She could do this. It was a done deal, JW finally owned his John Deere. He may not have time to use it, but he owned it.

Things were beginning to take shape. Household repairs were being made. JW and one of his friends replaced the leaky roof on the chicken coop one Saturday. The recent on going storms had taken a toll on the already aging roof. Roofing had been repaired so many times that there was nothing left to nail back on. It was leaking like a sieve. It had to be attended to now, repairs could not wait for over a year until his return.

They tore off the entire roof throwing the old roofing and wood into the work trailer. After that they put new sheets of plywood in place. Roofing material was rolled out to be nailed on top of the wood. Another huge task was completed by sunset that Saturday.

In the meantime, Bunny had worked on getting the house repairs started. The outside repairs were finished. The siding on the front of the house had been completely removed, damaged wood had been torn out with repair pieces nailed into place. A sheet of protective plastic had been installed before the siding was carefully replaced. Bunny had painted the shutters a bright white before the siding crew hung them back. She was waiting on the drywall team to show up for the inside work to begin.

It was going well until one afternoon when JW and Bunny returned from shopping to find another small problem. In their absence the strong wind gusts they'd faced all day had blown the double front window completely out of the frame. It was found in the middle of the living room floor. They looked at each other in total shock.

"I'll get the duct tape. You hold the window in place," was all that Bunny could say. She had learned long ago a roll of duct tape could fix almost anything.

"I don't believe this," was all JW could say as he pushed the window into place.

Another call to the insurance adjuster and contractor would have to be made to add this to the list of storm damages. On the bright side, it happened before the inside work was done. No water had to be mopped up this time since they got home before it rained.

While they waited for a new window to be ordered and installed, another storm accompanied by lightning burned out the garage door opener, all the phones, and the answering machine. Bunny was really beginning to hate the sound of impending storms. Of course, as the contractor was putting in the new opener he found a lot of other things wrong with the door. It needed some spring adjustments; bearings were bad, and a list of multiple problems completed the estimate. Not wanting to leave anything to chance, they had the entire door overhauled.

With the purchase of new phones and an answering machine, the total expense was just under the $500 deductible they carried on homeowners insurance. That was going to come directly out of their pocket. She could feel the money trickling out of the bank account at a rapid rate, money that they really needed to be saving.

The next thing to go was the faucet in the sink of the master bathroom. Early one morning she turned it on to find water spraying everywhere. This also caused it to leak into the cabinet below. Wonderful, more water related issues. She was ready to learn the backstroke just to be on the safe side. After their attempts to repair the thing several times, Bunny just simply gave up; a plumber was called to fix it. She was tired of problems, and really getting tired of mopping up water all the time.

To avoid any other water problems, a new battery was purchased for the back up sump pump in the basement in case the power went out. They had found out the hard way that a back up pump was a needed item when one had a basement and lived in the country.

One morning several years after moving into their dream home, they woke to find the power had gone out. Without the electric pump, water had continued to back up in the basement for most of the night. They had 4" of water in the basement by the time they realized they had a problem. Shortly after that the plumber installed a second battery operated pump to avoid that from happening again. It proved to be well worth the investment on more than one occasion. JW replaced the battery to assure Bunny that she didn't have to worry about replacing that, or bail water.

By the beginning of April, Bunny was exhausted and irritable all the time. She was constantly snapping at JW for any reason, or no reason at all. She was tired of balancing work, and all the other tasks she faced. She needed to be home instead of at work.

JW was sick and tired of hearing about it. He begged her to quit. She just could not handle all of this anymore. Something had to give, so in mid April she handed in her two weeks notice. She thought about asking for a leave of absence, but in her position it was all or nothing, so she just quit. Now she could devote her time to getting JW ready to leave, and get her house put back together. Without the stress of her job, perhaps life would become a bit easier. Once things calmed down in a few months, she would look into getting another job.

All of her energy was put into getting things pulled together. After weeks of waiting her window came in, only to find that during shipping it had been broken. Another delay before the window was finally replaced. This one proved to be watertight and windproof. She was getting the hang of mowing with the new tractor. It was as Bunny put it "blonde" user friendly. She would be able keep up the yard with this new green machine.

They cleaned up the yard, loading the burning barrels into the trailer with the roofing from the hen house to take to the dump. All of the recycled trash including papers, aluminum cans, plastic, and tin were dropped off at the recycling station. JW made sure the oil changes were all up to date in everything. The used oil was left at the auto shop to recycle. Three new barrels for trash burning were bought. JW placed them out back for her, which would get her through until next spring or summer.

Only a few more problems remained to be solved. How was she to lift the feedbags and gas cans out of the truck? Then once she got the gas cans out, how was she going to fill the tanks on the tractors? JW solved both dilemmas with a trip to the hardware store. He found a pulley system to hang on the rafters near the back of the work shed. All Bunny had to do was back the truck in, lower the tailgate, tie the gas can or the feed bag to the rope and pull. It took hardly any effort. Once the cargo cleared the tailgate, it was simple. The gas cans were lowered onto a small wooden cart with rollers that she could roll up to the tractor. He had bought a hand crank fuel transfer pump to siphon the fuel from the can into the tractor's tank. All of this could be done with no lifting involved.

The feed could be moved to the bucket loader on the tractor and driven out to the henhouse. From here she could dip it out into buckets to transfer to the bin inside the chicken coop. Bunny would not have to lift anything over her weight limit. It was ingenious of him to think of all of this for her. Now she could take care of the property while being able to keep her beloved critters, and continue to maintain her independence.

A chance meeting on a shopping trip one afternoon brought a dear friend back into Bunny's life. They had worked together in an office, which seemed like a lifetime ago. Bunny had been Jackie's supervisor, but they soon became much more than that. After Bunny left that job, she slowly lost track of her. Now here she was preparing to move close to her. She had purchased a lovely home in the same town Bea lived in. They'd almost be neighbors. Plans were set up to meet for lunch soon. Little did either one of them know that Jackie would be inducted into Bunny's team of warriors.

In May they both went to the Armory together on a drill weekend to get the final paperwork done. Bunny followed JW into the spacious room where the Army lawyers had tables lined up waiting for each Soldier to complete the needed documents. Piles of papers and files were scattered all around them. They were in the process of making out wills and power of attorney forms. Every aspect of this trip had to be addressed, even the unpleasant ones. The forms were for the "just in case" scenario. Bunny didn't want to think the unthinkable. JW had the lawyer draw up the power of attorney giving her total unlimited power over everything.

"Sir, are you sure you want to give her unlimited power of attorney? I've seen cases where that has been done. The Soldier comes home to find he owns nothing. The wife sells everything, splits leaving nothing behind, and it's totally legal," he stated with a tone of caution in his voice.

"Yep, that's exactly what I want. She really has everything anyway. This just makes it legal." JW said proudly entrusting his wife with all he owned. JW winked at his stunned wife. He smiled down at her as the printer churned out page after page of documents for signatures.

"You already own my heart. Why not give you everything else," he leaned down to whisper to her.

Bunny was overwhelmed with his faith in her. Never would she do anything in her life to betray his trust. She would do her very best to make sure everything was kept in order until his return.

With the major problems solved they could relax, working on the small stuff like personal items including clothing he would need for the coming year. They thought they had it licked until JW took the Jeep in to have a mechanic check on a noise coming from the rear of the vehicle. It was early June now. He had no time to mess with a break down on the road, definitely no time to complete any needed repairs. He didn't want to leave it for Bunny either. The repairs cost a little over $200, but it was worth it to just have it done.

JW was breathing a sigh of relief too soon. He put the window down on his way home from the shop that afternoon. The whole window lowered with a crash.

As Bunny turned into the drive he met her with a groan, "Don't get out of the car. I just broke the window on the Jeep. We have to go back to town to a glass repair shop now."

He had called literally begging the owner at the glass shop to fix the window. It turned out to be a bad regulator that controlled the power to raise and lower the window. They could have it done the next day if it was left with them that evening. It would cost another $200.

On the way in to pick it up the following day JW wearily requested, "Please promise me you won't break anything else until I'm gone. I can't stand to deal with one more thing before I go."

Trying her best to cheer him up she said, "Well, if anything else breaks I won't tell you. I'll just hide it," he nodded his head in agreement trying to find the strength to laugh.

Handling all of this was enough to stress them both to the max during the past few months. So, to get away from it all every weekend that they could, they would rise early to be on the new bicycle trail for an early morning ride. Some mornings they rode all the way to the nearest town making the round trip a good 12 miles. On each trip they saw various spring wildflowers in bloom, and songbirds in the massive trees that lined the trail. They loved to stop on a little bridge to watch ducks paddling in the murky water, or lazy turtles sunning on half submerged logs.

Several times they packed granola bars to eat for breakfast at one of their stops. Sometimes on the way home JW would stop to buy her one of her favorite, flavored coffees. He always surprised her with something. They looked forward to the weekends. The time spent together lifted the weight of the deployment from their world, if even for a short time. Those bike rides were important to both of them.

JW was trying to take it all in before his trip to the desert where everything was going to be the same shade of brown. They bought him a digital camera and a lap top computer to use on his trip overseas. Photos of everyone, and everything he could find to remind him of home were downloaded on the computer. He was going take a little bit of home with him since he had to go. He was sure in the months to come these few images would bring him comfort in the strange surroundings with the heat of the desert.

June had arrived too soon, and gone by too swiftly for both of them. It was nearing the end of the month now. Everything he would need for the next 15 months was stowed away in a footlocker, two duffle bags, and two small packs. He hoped that he had covered everything at home. If not, Bunny would have to find a way to get by because they were heading north for his final trip to the Armory that morning. She was trying to be brave about it all when inside she felt like she wanted to curl up and bawl her eyes out. These feeling had to be kept at bay; he needed her to be strong. Bunny wasn't about to let him down.

They tried to keep the conversation light and upbeat. It was Friday morning, time to drop him off at the Armory. She would return home that day, leaving him there to prepare for the trip to the training site. For the next three days the troops would be on lock down each evening.

She refused to let her spirits fall as she kissed him goodbye that morning. She knew that she would be returning to see him the next day as they held the final family support group meeting before they left.

She arrived early enough to help place centerpieces and balloons on the linen covered tables. JW joined her, and they sat together in silence holding hands though the meeting. A couple of times tears broke through as she quickly brushed them away, so JW wouldn't catch her crying.

After the meeting everyone was invited to a cookout hosted by a local construction company. It was their way of saying thanks to the troops and their families. Huge platters of grilled, juicy, steaks awaited them. A large buffet table lined with a delicious array of foods accompanied them for all to enjoy. Bunny and JW joined the other Soldiers and families in the party like atmosphere to partake of the meal. She was thankful for the people that provided her another opportunity to share a meal with her husband. Leaving him that evening proved to be more of a challenge than the farewell just a day earlier had been. Time was growing very short; they both knew every minute counted.

Tomorrow was to be the last hurrah. A deployment ceremony would be held in the gym of a local high school. All the families, friends, and most of the town would be there. On Sunday Bunny tried to look her best. She didn't want him to remember her in a T-shirt and blue jeans, so she'd pick a tropical blue, print dress with matching blue sandals. She had spent extra time on her hair and makeup. He commented on how beautiful he thought she looked. She was far from being a super model, but he always made her feel like she was the only woman on the planet.

He loved her blonde hair. He could gaze deeply into her green eyes that sparkled with just a hint of mischief to melt his heart. He truly enjoyed her laughter, and the life they shared. She needed him to focus on these things to get him through the rough times ahead. She would keep her focus on him to get past the obstacles she would face alone.

Bunny's mom and dad made the two-hour trip from their house to see him off that day. They weren't about to have him leave without a final farewell. Bunny told Mick and Leann to stay at home. They didn't want Leann to have to suffer the stress of the ride along with heat only to have the baby arrive too soon. Besides, they had privately said their goodbyes to JW earlier. Leann had written letter for him. It included Psalms 91, a promised prayer of protection, a letter he would carry with him to comfort him through the long months ahead.

The gym was crowded and very hot. All the Soldiers marched in as the crowd stood to their feet to cheer. She was proud, yet sad at the same time, proud for what he believed in, sad because he had to leave her because of it. The ceremony ended with the troops being dismissed until 9pm. They had a few precious hours to go before she would have to leave. Bunny's folks left tearfully for the long drive home. That gave the two of them time alone to say goodbye.

With spirits high he took her to a BBQ place quite a drive away from the Armory, so they could be away from the crowds. It would be many lonely months before she would be sitting down to dinner with him again. They enjoyed the meal, then sat at the table like two lovesick teenagers until he decided they needed to head back. Bunny was stuck to him like a leech, not wanting to let go for fear he would vanish into thin air.

They spent a little time in the picnic area in back of the building to visit with a few of the other troops. At 8 pm JW ushered her toward the car, they would go on lockdown at 9. He wanted her on the road soon. It was tearing at their hearts to know that the deadline was so near. They hugged and kissed each other knowing that time was running out. In the morning the troops would be herded onto buses that would take them to the airport flying them to their training site.

A big citywide send off was planned for the next morning, but JW didn't want Bunny to make the trip back for it. She would not be able to even get close to him. He asked her not to come to the event. She was relieved knowing that she did not have to idly stand on a street corner waving a flag while he drove past her taking her heart with him. She fought back the emotions welling up inside her. Tears formed in her eyes as she attempted to keep them at bay without success. Bravely she blew kisses to him through the open car window while proclaiming her love for him.

She waved and whispered, "Goodbye, my love."

Then she headed out the drive. Looking in the rear view mirror, she could see his silhouette standing in the drive watching her drive slowly out of sight. His image was set in her mind. She began the long road home to a lonely house.

It didn't take long for tears to stream steadily down her cheeks. She wouldn't stop the car, if she did she would never make it home. She had to keep moving, or the dam holding back the flood of tears would break to wash her away in a tidal wave of emotions. The trip home seemed to have no end. Every mile of the road was torture taking her farther away from her love.

Finally, she parked the car in the garage. Wearily, she stepped out into her new life. She closed the door to the house behind her dreading the dawn of the next day, her first day without him, the first of many to come. She carefully placed the program from the ceremony on a table in the extra room that held his remaining Army items. She stood in the middle of the nearly empty room. She looked around at the line of black boots, and outdated BDU uniforms hanging in the partially open closet door. The freshly shined boots and starched uniforms stood like proud Soldiers awaiting orders.

The scent of shoe polish filled the air as she traced his name with her fingers on a uniform. She thumbed through the uniforms and closed her eyes. A mental picture of him came into focus. She could see him wearing that uniform with pride, dignity, and honor. They were the qualities that made him the man she loved. He was gone from her side, but he would always occupy her heart.

She closed the door behind her making her way down the long hall to bed. Exhausted and weeping she lay awake for hours replaying the past three days in her mind. The last few meals, the sound of his laughter, his blue, soul searching eyes all more than mere memories to store away. It was well into the night before she found rest.

The sun still rose the next morning, but in her world it was dark and gloomy. She knew that her beloved husband was being shoved onto a bus this morning and carted off. Why had she allowed him to talk her into not seeing him leave? She regretted that decision even though she knew that being there would have only extended the pain of letting him go. Besides, he was a Captain, and he needed to concentrate on his troops now instead of worry about her. He had a job to do. Her being there wouldn't have accomplished anything. She lay in the big empty bed, content to wallow in self-pity long after she should have been up. Reluctantly, she picked up the ringing phone.

Beatrice asked way too cheerfully, "You up?"

"I'm awake, but I am not happy about it," Bunny snorted.

"Come on you have to get going. Besides, I'm coming out to see you. I have something for you," she sounded way too eager to visit.

"What?" Bunny wanted to know.

"Can't tell you. I have to show you. I'm coming out...get dressed," Bea hung up the phone before Bunny could protest.

Before she was completely ready to face anyone, including her best friend the doorbell rang. Bea must have broken the sound barrier to get here that fast Bunny thought as she ran down the stairs. She had flung on a pair of wrinkled jeans and a tattered shirt. Twisting her hair up in a ponytail, she opened the front door to find a huge bouquet of long stemmed red roses being thrust at her.

"Special delivery!" an excited Bea shouted.

Bunny was speechless, which didn't happen often, "Who are they from?" Bunny asked.

Laughing Bea said, "Well Duh! JW sent them to my house to have me bring them to you. He didn't want you to be alone today, so here I am."

Bunny grabbed an armload of flowers and friend to pull them into the kitchen. Both of their faces were wet with tears of joy and sorrow. They admired the roses while Bunny filled her friend in on the events of the past several days. She was blessed to have a husband like this; blessed to have a friend to be there just as she promised she would be.

Her parents and in-laws called concerned about her welfare. Jackie checked in to set up a luncheon date. Mick and Leann called to check on her, knowing that this was her first day alone. Leann comforted her by praying with her for strength and comfort. JW was leaving for the training site today, but he had left her in good hands. The day ended on a much higher note than it began because of the people in her life that loved her.

A few days later a phone call from JW confirmed that he had reached his destination. The Army wanted everyone to call home to let their families know they were there, and all was well. It was short and sweet, but welcomed by Bunny just to hear his voice again. It seemed like ages since she had last heard his laughter. He was in good spirits, just glad to have finally gotten the process started.

CHAPTER THREE

During the rest of June and July Bunny tried to keep busy. She finished crocheting the two baby blankets for Leann's upcoming shower. A large, crib size, yellow one and a smaller, green, one were completed for the baby. A white sweater and booties set were knitted. They were all quickly wrapped in tissue paper in a large box. She bought items for the baby every time she went shopping. They were the small things they would need on visits to grandma's house. Friends and family kept invitations flowing. Her brothers and sister-in laws kept cards, phone calls, and emails of encouragement flowing to her. There had been Leann's baby shower, Sunday dinners, Mustang Club meetings, car cruises, and numerous picnics. She even managed to go to a 4th of July outing without having a total meltdown.

Bea and Jackie were around to keep her occupied during the summer. Bea had finished with her teaching job for the summer, and Jackie had moved to her new home. Bunny could usually find one of them free to shop with, grab a bite in town, or visit with when she needed company. They helped her hang onto her sanity.

She accompanied Leann on one of the prenatal visits. Bunny was overjoyed to hear the sound of her little grandchild when they heard the child's heartbeat. Leann would soon bring this precious, new life into the world. The doctor told her she was going to have a boy. They were very happy that he was healthy, and Leann was doing well. Mick was on cloud nine. The news was quickly relayed to JW in an email that a grandson was on the way.

Bunny and Leann finished shopping for the remaining items she would need for the baby. They bought a tan backpack-baby bag so Mick wouldn't feel out of place carrying it. It looked like a backpack, not a diaper bag. The sales clerk said it was a top seller, very popular among the young fathers. It allowed the parents to sling it on their back leaving both hands free to attend to the baby. The neutral color and design would encourage use long after the baby stage was over. Mick and Leann could use it on trips later as the child grew. It would be prefect for them.

Mick had assembled the crib. All the bedding was put into place in anticipation of the new arrival. Leann had all the clothes and supplies laid in for the baby. Now they just had to wait until Jack made his entrance.

The drywall team finally finished their work. Bunny began painting the living room. In fact, she picked out a new color scheme for the entire downstairs with Bea's help. Redecorating would be her therapy. The key to coping with JW absence was to keep going until she was too tired to think. At night it was all she could do to make it to bed, by the end of the day she was totally exhausted. Even then sleep did not come to her easily.

It was early in July when Bunny got her first email from JW, for the next 15 months they would use email to stay in contact. Cards and letters would be exchanged, too. In one of the many classes given before the Soldiers left home, the families were told to keep the flow of information to their Soldiers positive. They were going to be stressed to their limits and beyond. If they couldn't do anything about a given situation, they need not know about it.

Bunny had to make sure that she portrayed her life as being full of rainbows, butterflies, and fluffy bunnies at all times. Whatever problems came her way, it was up to the good Lord and her to solve.

Her messages to him were about the activities in her life, minus anything unpleasant, things were kept light. She always ended with a love note. She never wanted JW to forget her love for him.

JW's emails tapered off by the end of July. They were training all the time now. Bunny continued to send brief daily reports from home, one or two lines to update him on her routine. When he could pick them up, he would know that he had been in her thoughts every day.

July passed quickly into August. Bunny had set up a routine to help her adjust to her new life. She was always up by 5:30 every day, either stirred from her slumber by the "alarm cat" wanting to be fed, or by her own inner clock. She would drag herself from bed, then dress always remembering to wear the simple pewter cross JW had given her before he left. It was a simple Celtic cross on a piece of green cord that matched one he wore around his neck beside his dog tags. It was her link to his heart, and their faith that God's protection would pour out upon them. She then turned to a time for devotion and prayer before attempting to start anything.

Needing to keep busy, she threw herself into other chores at home. Two days were spent washing, removing road oil, and waxing the Jeep and Mustang. The interiors got the best cleaning they had ever known, every inch was polished and shined. She was patting herself on the back for being able to cope so well when she found a pair of JW's lost sunglasses that had slipped unnoticed under the driver's seat of the Jeep. Caught totally off guard by the discovery she held them close to heart, sat in the middle of the garage floor, and cried for what seemed to be hours.

She found it was small moments like this that brought a flood of tears to her eyes. Moments during a major crisis were handled better because she knew she had to march on to get things done. There was no time to break down, only time for action. Little problems seemed to be the straw that broke the camel's back, like the afternoon she stopped for lunch to make a peanut butter and jelly sandwich. As hard as she tried the lid would not budge from the jar on the peanut butter.

Each turn of the lid left her more frustrated until finally, she opened the back door to throw it into the yard, where it remained for two days before she retrieved it. Flinging it out the back door didn't open the jar, but it made Bunny feel better by doing it.

Early on the morning of the 24th of August Bunny got a call from Mick. He was calm, but urgent, "Mom we are going to the hospital. Leann is in labor, and the doctor told us to get things ready. We need to go in."

The baby was over a week late. Every day she had waited for this call to come. Mick and Leann had been hoping for labor to begin for days. They were more than ready to meet their son, Leann more than Mick at this point.

"Do you want me to meet you there? It may take awhile for things to happen. I could be there to give you a break," she asked.

"If you want to that would be great mom. We just don't want to interrupt your day," Mick sounded relieved for the offer. It would not be an interruption to her day it was a blessing, one that they had waited on for months.

Bunny showered quickly, packed a bag with a few snacks, and an extra change of clothes. She got to the hospital as Mick and Leann arrived at 11am. Leann was checked in, and sent to the maternity ward. They were put in a delivery suite much different than when Bunny had given birth to Mick. Labor and delivery took place all in the same room. They would let the father stay with mother and baby the entire time until they were sent home together as a family.

As the day progressed, labor intensified. The decision to have natural childbirth without drugs was tossed aside a few hours before delivery. Contractions were coming closer together after the doctor ordered a drug to induce a quicker delivery. That really got things moving along.

Unable to keep up with the intense labor Leann gave in to make the demand, "I want drugs…NOW." Which made nurses scatter to fulfill her request.

Bunny told them she would leave to wait in the lounge if they wanted her out of the way for the delivery. Leann wanted help from Mick, her sisters, mom, and Bunny. She was there when little Jack came into the world. It was a long labor, but in the end at 12:20 am on the morning of the 25th Jack arrived. He was a healthy baby boy, weighing in at 9 pounds 8 ounces, and 21 inches long with thick, dark, brown hair. He was a full two pounds larger than the doctor had predicted he would be. He was beautiful, and such a blessing. Bunny wished that JW could be there to hold the precious bundle.

Everyone stayed for several hours to marvel at the beautiful child, lending support to the new parents. Jack lay sleeping in Bunny's arms when Leann's sister asked when JW would be home to see Jack.

"He may not meet him until he's over a year old," Bunny told her. As soon as Bunny had spoken those words, Jack woke up screaming.

Leann sat up promptly questioning, "What's wrong with my baby?"

"All I did was ask when JW would get to see him. Bunny told me that he might be a year old before they met, then out of the blue Jack started screaming. He knows, Jack knows his grandpa is not here," her sister told Leann as Bunny comforted the baby now asleep again in her arms.

Bunny gave Jack back to Leann. "I don't know if that has anything to do with him crying or not. But, just in case we won't mention the fact that his Grandpa is in Iraq," Leann stated.

Again, Jack woke from his slumber screaming when the conversation turned to his grandfather. Leann held the baby tight whispering softly to him, "That's ok, your grandpa loves you, he will hold you very soon."

Jack snuggled in his blankets, the crying stopped as quickly as it had started, and he slept. Could he have known JW wasn't there?

Bunny called to leave a message for JW about the baby's birth. They were all certain that everyone within earshot of him that day would know he had just become a Grandpa. Everyone on post would be getting a cigar to celebrate; he'd already assured them of that.

It was a month of blessings. Bunny got a call from Tracey that brought good news. Tracey and Bunny had become close friends during the past months. They had exchanged phone numbers early in their budding friendship. Even though they lived in different parts of the state, they contacted each other often for support.

"What you doin'?" the familiar greeting rang in her ears when Bunny picked up the phone.

"Just waiting on you to call," Bunny replied.

"Have you heard the news?" Tracey asked.

"News of what?" she wanted to know.

"The guys get to go on leave. The end of the month they get 4 to 5 days off. And, they can have company!" she exclaimed.

"You aren't kidding me are you? Because if you are, I will hunt you down and torture you," Bunny was hoping the information was true.

"I'm not joking. It's true. So, you want to go see your man or what?" Tracey kidded her.

"I'm packing now," Bunny shouted. The two of them began planning the trip out east with enthusiasm to see their husbands.

A call from JW was the next to come in. It was true. She could come out to see him. Their spirits were soaring as they made plans to meet. It would mean a long drive, Bunny didn't fly the friendly skies very well. It wasn't that she was afraid to fly. It was because it never failed to make her ill, something to do with motion sickness. That meant she always got a full row to herself though, if the plane had empty seats, because she sat in her seat with one of those little white bags on her lap the entire trip. No matter what medication she took to avoid it, the outcome was always the same. No one wanted to sit next to that.

Sense of direction was not a gift Bunny had been blessed with. It was settled that Bunny would drive the Jeep. Tracey who was good with details would be the navigator. Tracey researched the routes they would take. A meeting place was set up for Bunny to pick her up on the way, then they'd be off on their adventure. The Jeep needed an oil change and tire rotation before the trip. Bunny took it in to the shop, and waited for the job to be done.

A mechanic walked up to her while the vehicle was still up on the rack, this could mean only trouble. He informed her that everything checked out, but...oh, there was that word again. But, the brakes were shot. God, please don't let it be expensive! Already on a strict budget, Bunny could see her plans of going east fading. She had not gotten a job yet, so money was still tight. The young man stepped behind the counter. He began tapping away on the keyboard of the office computer.

He looked up smiling, "You aren't going to believe this. You had these brakes put on here, right? They are two weeks away from the warranty running out. We'll replace them at no charge."

Thank God! With the Jeep given the all clear to travel, and money still in her pocket for the trip hopes were running high again. She could continue with her plans.

Mick, Leann, and Jack were home from the hospital. Bunny had prepared their first dinner for them knowing that they would be bone tired after the trek home. She laid out the baked chicken dinner, volunteering to watch Jack while they ate undisturbed. Bunny visited them as often as she could without feeling like she was butting in. They always welcomed her visits though.

Mick had saved his vacation time to adjust to their new role as parents. The three of them were doing well. Bunny felt comfortable in leaving to see JW. With everything in order, and a pocket full of photos to share with grandpa she could go.

On the last day of August Bunny and Tracey met. They stuffed their suitcases, a cooler, and a few snacks into the red Jeep. Off for the open road they headed. Most of the trip would be made in the dark of night. They hoped traffic would be lighter then than traveling in the peak daytime hours. Frequent stops had to be made, or by the time they arrived at the end of their journey Bunny's back wouldn't allow her to move. Tracey didn't seem to mind. They soon fell into a lighthearted conversation that carried them through the entire trip.

Tracey had under estimated the time they would reach their destination. She missed an entire page of directions, and then assumed they were closer than they actually were. Arriving 3 hours later than expected, they found their husbands waiting for them in a rental van just inside the main gate. Bunny parked the Jeep to run into JW's waiting arms. It felt so good to have him hold her again. It was difficult to let him go long enough to get back into the vehicle to get to the room.

In all the preparation for the trip, no one had thought of getting the reservations for the motel rooms on post. JW had gone to the office earlier that day to find they had only one room for the night. Thankfully, it had two queen size beds. For that first night, which was almost over by now, the couples shared a room. Everyone was so exhausted that each couple dropped onto a bed, and quickly fell asleep holding their spouse next to them at last. Bunny had no problem falling asleep that night wrapped in JW's arms.

The next morning John and JW had things to attend to at "0 dark thirty." It gave the wives a chance to sleep in an hour or two longer before they had to be up. They had slept in the clothes they had arrived in, and welcomed the chance to get settled into their own rooms. JW was the first to return with hot coffee and pastries. As soon as they ate, they were off for the motel office to square away the housing issue. After checking out of the room they had just left, the motel clerk tried to book the three of them into one room. JW explained that they needed two rooms, for two couples this time. For some reason the poor clerk thought that Bunny and Tracey were both JW's wives.

"One wife is all I can handle. This one belongs to someone else," JW joked pointing to Tracey.

The three of them nearly rolled on the floor in laughter after the previous night's sleep deprivation. After an hour of explanations, canceling charges on credit cards, and rerunning the billing correctly, they had two rooms, one for Tracey and her spouse, John, the other for Bunny and JW. They parted to go their separate ways until time for them to head home.

Luggage was unloaded into the new room. Bunny and JW took

quick showers to freshen up. A call was placed for a pizza delivery. JW found the home baked apple pie that Bunny had carefully packed. Lovingly she had picked the apples from the trees on the back of the property. It had been baked early the day she left, and was still warm when she had packed it into the Jeep. She wanted to take him a taste of home to enjoy. He tore into the pie long before the pizza arrived.

The rest of the day was spent in talking about progress on the house, tidbits of news from home, and Jack. She gave him a small book filled with photos of baby Jack. He poured over each picture of his grandson and the kids. He commented on how healthy and happy they all looked.

He couldn't tell her much about what his world had been like, other than to make the comment that it had been rough. They had been out training in the pouring rain, and the heat of the summer sun. He was bone tired. He needed a rest from the vigorous, non-stop training schedule. They fell asleep cuddled up watching an old movie on TV. It was late in the afternoon when they woke.

Leftover pizza and apple pie was the main course for supper. Snacks from the picnic basket Bunny had packed made for a late night treat. They once again fell asleep in front of the TV.

The next few days went by way too fast. One day was spent on a nearby beach. No one was allowed to swim because of the high winds, and huge waves crashing onto the shore. Since they were already there, they just took off their shoes to walk at the waters edge letting the sand squeeze between their toes. The sun felt wonderfully warm as the wind blew strong enough to top the waves with bubbly, white caps. They held hands, and laughed feeling carefree for the first time in months.

Bunny playfully teased him that she should take a photo of him surrounded by some of the bathing beauties. He could show them to the troops that planned on hanging out, and moping around the post for length of the entire leave. He dared her to do it, the game was on. She found three attractive young gals leisurely soaking up the sun.

"Excuse me, I was wondering if you could do me a favor?" Bunny asked boldly. That got their attention. "See that guy in the light orange polo shirt down there? That's my husband, he's going to be shipped over seas soon. His buddies back at the barracks refused to come to the beach with us today. I was wondering if you would pose for a couple photos with him, so he can show them what are missing."

They looked in JW's direction and one said, "Hey, he's cute."

Looking at her two friends, they nodded in agreement. "Sure we'll do it," they said standing up giggling.

They followed Bunny down to JW. He looked up just in time to see her little procession greet him at the water's edge. The look on his face was priceless. Introductions were made as Bunny took charge to prepare for the photo shoot.

Bunny announced, "Now feel free to hang all over him, I want some good pictures." They readily complied with her request.

A series of photos were taken to assure her that she had at least a couple of good shots. Bunny thanked them as they ran back to their beach towels quite proud of themselves for their part in the whole affair.

As payback, JW had her pose on the shoreline while he shot several pictures of her as the waves lapped at her feet. He kept telling to back up for each shot so he could get the waves in the picture. She fell for it hook, line, and sinker. A huge wave came in totally soaking her up to her shoulders. Bunny shook her finger at him, scolding him for being so cruel, unable to keep from laughing the entire time even though it would take several hours for her clothes to dry out.

That afternoon JW downloaded several photo of him with the bikini clad gals to email to the stick in mud troops telling them they needed to get out. He was still amazed at the way Bunny had talked the girls into posing for the pictures. She reminded him that he hadn't put up much of a protest to the idea though. The fact that he was grinning from ear to ear in each photo proved her point. She was certain that every rental car on post would be headed for the beach the next day in search of adventure and the three bathing beauties.

They had supper at a quaint little seafood café that evening. They ordered Cajun crab, garlic crab and spicy boiled crab for appetizers, JW ordered a fish platter, and Bunny got coconut shrimp with the works. It was wonderful sitting near the beach eating fresh seafood. For a short time they forgot about every one and every thing, except each other. He had a way of sweeping her off her feet even after all these years of marriage.

He took her to the shops in the mall and PX on post one day. They bought a few gifts for Mick and Leann. Bunny found JW in the toy section looking at little red wagons and blue tricycles. She steered him to a baby section where they selected more age appropriate gifts for Jack. He was so proud of his new grandson. It was a fun filled day. They were marveling in just being together.

They hit the clearance rack finding all types of wonders. JW picked a purple, beaded, fairy wand with feathers and ribbons hanging from it out of a box of last year's left over Halloween items. He looked ridiculous holding it. Bunny was totally amused by his antics.

"I wish I'd found this earlier, I could have used it in the field," he remarked. He ceremoniously waved it over her head, tapping her on both shoulders. "Your world is a wonderful and beautiful place. All of your problems have disappeared, you have been touched by the anti-griping wand. Go forth, be happy, and gripe no more."

As they both laughed a Colonel rounded the corner to ask if they had any left. He needed one for his next staff meeting. Soon everyone was purchasing fairy wands.

A trip to the zoo took them away for a day. They spent the day strolling from one animal to the next taking candid snapshots on the way. Bunny got a good one of a llama "kissing" JW on the cheek. He in turn snapped one of her feeding the giraffes.

She had him take a picture of her with her hand in the snarling mouth of a stuffed wolf in the gift shop while she faked a scream for fun. It made other visitors in the room burst out in uncontrollable laughter as they strolled by.

"Please don't encourage her," JW said as he laughed along with them.

He made the comment of how much he missed the critters at home. Inside the main building he got the chance to pet a few cats and dogs before they left, which only made him more homesick for Larkin and Goldie, if that were possible.

All too soon it was over, the troops had to go back. Bunny and Tracey dropped JW and John off at their barracks. They made the goodbyes quick to ease the pain of leaving. The Jeep headed toward the front gate. On the way home, Tracey received a call from John, which made the return trip home a joyful one.

"Wait, slow down. You have got to be kidding me," she looked at Bunny. "They have just been told that they have another 5 day pass next weekend. We can see them again if you want to make the drive."

"Count me as good as there," Bunny's heart was soaring. One more chance to visit her husband before he shipped out. There wasn't much time left, she would walk through fire to hold him one more time before he had to go.

Tracey and John babbled on for a few moments as Bunny's brain was already planning the next trip. She would have to ask Bea and Slick to care for the animals again. She would need to restock and repack her bags. Oh, happy days.

Bunny got home late Tuesday night. The drive home had taken 16 hours, her body felt every mile of it now. Her spirits were on cloud nine, even if her body was aching. On the way home after dropping Tracey off, she had called Bea.

"It's me. I am almost home from my epic journey," she told her.

"Are you okay? I have been thinking about you all day coming home after having to say goodbye and all," Bea said.

"I'm fine. Well, more than fine really. You see he gets a second pass next week. I want to go back out to see him if you can manage the farm again," Bunny chattered on in one endless breath.

Bea was more than thrilled to hear that the trip had been a good one. She volunteered to do the chores again for her friend. All was set into motion for the next week. Jackie's contact information was given to Bea for backup help in case the workload was a burden.

As Bunny was doing laundry to prepare for the second trip, she received a frantic call from her dad on September 11th. Mom had been ill all morning. She had taken three nitro tablets for chest pains earlier that morning, but his time the nitro didn't stop the pain like usual. An ambulance had to be called to take her to the hospital. Bunny met her father in the emergency room. The doctors confirmed that mom had suffered another heart attack. Tests were run before it was decided that surgery was out of the question. Blockage that she had was in an area where they couldn't "balloon" it out. She had lost 25% of her heart muscle this time, she was too weak for surgery. The only thing they could do was control it with medication. She would have to stay in the hospital for possibly a week to get things under control.

Bunny was supposed to leave in two days. How could she leave her mom like this, and travel that far away? She talked to the entire family that had assembled at Mom's bedside. Everyone was in agreement that the trip out east should go on as planned on the 13th, they would care for mom, she was told to go.

She was torn between staying at her mother's bedside, and going to see her husband again. The battle waged on in her heart and mind. She was going to feel guilt no matter what she decided. Finally, Bunny kissed her mom, telling her she would return in a few days. She left to pack for her journey carrying a heavy heart with her.

The trip on the 13th was more difficult than the previous one. Tracey had suffered from neck and upper back pain since they had returned just a week ago. She was in constant pain. Bunny was worn out from the past few days and nights spent at the hospital with her mom. The only saving grace was that on this trip Ellen, Tracey's daughter would accompany them. Ellen was in high school; she could drive if they need her to. They started off heading east again.

Ellen was as energetic and bubbly as her mother. Poor Tracey took pain medication, and curled up in the back seat to sleep as they sped on into the night. Ellen's main job was to keep Bunny from nodding off to sleep, killing them all in a fiery car crash. She supplied Bunny with cold soda, snacks, and lively conversation. She tuned in rock and roll stations on the radio. She did everything possible to keep her alert and awake.

Bunny failed to wake Tracey up for directions in time, a wrong exit took them off the route. Now, they had to make a course correction to get back on the right highway. They ended up lost and frustrated two more times before they finally spotted the gate to the military post. It was noon by the time the Jeep pulled into the lot where they were to meet JW and John. They weren't late this time even with all of the errors they'd made. Bunny had a lead foot this trip out.

The troops were dismissed for noon "chow", but told to report back afterwards. They could eat together with their families on post, and then report in. Burger King was the nearest place to eat, so they headed there quickly. Tracey grabbed a seat nearby as soon as the order was placed. Bunny plopped down beside her. JW and John were left to wait at the counter for the food. Both women were exhausted.

Bunny and Tracey looked awful, but explained it away by telling the men of all the travel mishaps. Bunny wasn't going to say a word about mom, Tracey planned on hiding her pain from John, Ellen was sworn to secrecy regarding both problems. The men looked like they were in need of rest and plenty of it. Napping away the rest of the day was in order.

Bunny was happy that the decision had been made to stay off post this time. Tracey had taken charge of room reservations on this trip. Rooms would be waiting for them in a town about 20 minutes from post. They needed to be away from everything Army. As soon as they were dismissed, John picked up a rental car for his family. Everybody then headed out for the motel to nap the rest of the afternoon away.

Having been given a second chance to be together, JW took Bunny off on a sight seeing tour for two days. They drove to see Independence Hall, where their great nation had been conceived. Photos were taken at the Liberty Bell, and he took her to China Town for lunch. They spent an entire day at Valley Forge, taking a ton of pictures.

It rained one whole day. They spent the entire day watching TV, munching on leftovers from a huge seafood dinner the night before, and cuddling in the warmth of each other's arms. On the morning of the 18th, the gals once again had to drop them off to head for home.

Both husbands had excess clothing and gear to send home. They packed duffle bags and boxes into the Jeep for their wives to take home to put in storage. If they couldn't take the unneeded items home, the men would have to find some way to ship them home. These were things that wouldn't be needed on the next part of their journey. The back of the Jeep was crammed full. One half of the back seat now held the women's suitcases. It was stuffed, but everything fit, leaving just enough room for the three women.

This was the final time for them to say goodbyes. The Jeep was soon on the way west, back home, back to life without him, this time for 12 months.

Every bone in her body screamed the morning after her return home, but she had to get up. She needed to check in at the hospital. Every muscle ached, her body cried out for more sleep. She had called home twice while JW was away from her for a few minutes during the week, but the calls were brief. The family told her to not worry that things were going well. She had to see for herself, she had to make sure mom was ok. If the medication was working then plans had to be made for her release from the hospital.

It was highly recommended by her doctors that they have some kind of help for a while. Mom needed regular monitoring from the visiting nurse and the occupational therapist.

This had been a close call, without the help of the paramedics, mom would not have made it this time. With their help she had barely pulled through to make it to the hospital. Bunny talked to her brothers at length. They lived out of state, and mom's doctors were here. It was only logical for mom and dad to stay with Bunny. She could monitor her health. Both brothers would be available when she needed their help. She wasn't working, her entire 24-hour day could be devoted to her care. It was the logical solution to the current problem they faced. Their father gladly accepted the help offered.

Bunny really needed their presence for her own comfort as well. She had always been close to her parents. They needed each other more than ever right now. JW and Bunny had been trying for years to get them to move into their big house. They were empty nesters with extra rooms to fill. She would welcome them into the lonely house gladly.

By mid week JW emailed home telling her that he would be on leave again the next weekend, but only for 3 days. Everyone would be required to remain on post this time. He would just rent a room at the motel on post and chill out alone. He had been in the field, so he would welcome unlimited long, hot, showers, and clean, fluffy, sheets. Besides, that he needed sleep. The barracks was always crowded and noisy, getting any rest there was out of the question.

He would love to see her again, but he could not go through the thought of yet another goodbye. He couldn't put her through it either. She was relieved that she didn't have to explain why she could not go to him if he had asked her to visit. Mom's heart attack could remain a secret at least for now. He promised to email her often. He would call home often over the weekend just to hear her voice.

Mom would not be able to climb the stairs to the bedroom, so Mick came over to moved the furniture around, making room for the guest bed to be moved into the living room. All of the painting and redecorating in the living room was done. Four days after Bunny returned from her latest trip, she was ready to have them come stay with her. Dad went home to pack a few clothes for their stay. He prepared their house for a long hibernation before turning the key in the lock of their once happy, little cottage, not sure if they would be returning any time soon.

Mom was weak, but happy to leave the hospital behind her for the comfort of her daughter's home. Dad and Bunny had a huge job ahead of them. A new schedule including all her new medications had to be set, meals and snacks had to be planned, visits to all her doctors must be made, appointments from visiting nurses, and occupational therapists needed to be scheduled. Bunny was glad to help in any way she could. She was really busy, which should have kept her mind from wandering to JW. Nothing could keep her from the daily concerns she felt for him.

JW was informed of the new arrivals in the household, just not given all the facts. She had never lied to him, she preferred to look at this as simply withholding a few of the details, in this case it was a lot of the details. He thought that the folks had moved in to keep her company for the winter. Whatever it took to keep him happy was fine with her. Remember, rainbows, butterflies, and fluffy bunnies!

Shortly after the monumental move, word came from JW that the unit was leaving for overseas soon. He couldn't say when, so if communications dropped off not to worry. He had called to hear her voice one last time. They both ended up chocking back emotions before the call ended. She placed the phone back on the receiver, and wept silently. He was going to be thousands of miles from home when she really needed him here. She needed the comfort of his reassuring presence, but she would not have him to lean on. Even with the overwhelming schedule, she managed to keep positive emails flowing into JW's account. Once he reached his destination, he would find them waiting patiently for him. Each one of them carried with it her love.

CHAPTER FOUR

It was during this chaotic period that the faucet in kitchen failed. Bunny found everything under the sink soaked with water. What was it with this whole destruction by water thing anyway? Well, she had to use it everyday, so everything stored under the sink was moved to a large box to be pushed into a corner. A bucket was placed under the leak to keep another flood at bay while she decided what to do.

The support group had promised help with household repairs in times of need while the Soldiers were gone. Well, this was a time of need. Bunny called to explain the situation, to plead for help. She was promised that a request would be forwarded through the proper channels. Now she would have to wait for a response.

A change had taken place in mom since her massive heart attack. She was confused a lot, the same questions were asked over and over again. She constantly complained that the room was dark even with all the lights on. She found it difficult to read the paper, and couldn't remember what she had just read. She was always requesting to know the time.

Bunny had confided to Bea that mom was beginning to drive her a little nuts. To lighten the mood; Bea would call to check on her daily, "What time is it?" became her new salutation.

"Daddy, doesn't momma ever get on your nerves?" Bunny had to ask one afternoon, Bunny wondered how dad could stand the constant bombardment of questions.

"What?" he said as he put his hands up to his hearing aids to adjust the volume.

"You cheater! You turn your 'ears' off," Bunny laughed at his solution to the problem.

In the first part of October, Bunny received her first email from her love overseas. He was in Kuwait. It had been only a couple of days since she had gotten that phone call from him in the states. He must have waited until the last possible moment to call her before he boarded the plane. Everyone was safe, and they would be in Kuwait for some time before moving on to Iraq. She continued to get emails before contact with him ceased two weeks later. After 4 days he informed her that he had reached his final destination somewhere in Iraq.

From the time JW left the states Bunny had been on pins and needles. She refused to watch the news programs. Every time a news story about a convoy hitting a roadside bomb flashed on the screen her heart sank. Was his unit involved? She even stopped taking the morning paper to avoid the articles that stared at her from the front page about the war in Iraq. She had enough on her plate right now to cope with, more stress created by these outside factors was the last thing she needed. She wasn't avoiding reality as one of her friends had accused her of, she was simply avoiding more stress.

On one of mom's better mornings she called Bunny to her side. It was before 5 am. Mom pulled her down on the bedside to sit next to her.

"What's wrong momma?" worry was apparent in Bunny's voice.

"Today is Sunday isn't it?" she asked.

"Yes, Momma, it's Sunday. Why?" Bunny answered used to questions of this nature.

"Because you need to go to church. Get ready, and wear your purple dress. Go to church. You need to go to church," was mom's command.

Bunny had been prompted to return to church by Leann shortly after JW left to go for training. She declined the offer several times before finally accepting. JW and Bunny had been "pew warmers" for many years, but not what one would call "on fire Christians." Leann and Mick seemed to be able to handle whatever life threw at them. They had found strength and peace, maybe she could also. She found what she was looking for in those church services. It was peace she needed in her life to help her deal with the turmoil raging inside her. She was finally able to hand her worries about JW, and her parent's health over to God. He was put in total control. Bunny remained concerned about issues, but not consumed by them any longer. She found the help she needed through loving caring fellow Christians.

It was during an altar call one Sunday morning, she rededicated her life to God. It was her renewed faith that carried her through these troubled times. It was faith that had helped her face all of the trials of the past months. God would get her through it all. God gave her the strength to face each day, one by one. He put the joy in her heart, and the smile on her face.

Bunny had been missing church services with the trips to see JW and mom's illness. She was being drained of her spiritual strength. Mom could sense it, and in a moment of lucidity sent her daughter to church to refill her spiritual tank.

During the next visit to the doctor, he confirmed what they already knew. Because of the lack of oxygen to her brain, mom's memory and eyesight had been affected. She may improve over time, but how much they couldn't tell. It was a test of patience for Bunny. She continued to treat mom with love and affection while caring for her even with raw nerves. 'Honor thy mother and thy father' ran through her mind constantly. Treating her disrespectfully would be breaking one of God's commandments.

Thankfully, Eugene, her oldest brother, called to announce that he would be coming up to give her a break. Everyone knew the tremendous pressure she was under. They had called often to offer moral support. The folks wanted desperately to return home.

Eugene's wife, Joan, would be with him to help them adjust to the new schedule. Joan was a wonderful cook. She would be able to prepare healthy meals for them, and supply a bountiful stockpile to be placed in the freezer for future use. The folks would be able to eat well-balanced meals once they were on their own again without the stress of cooking.

It was with mixed emotions that Bunny helped them pack to go. One look in the mirror told her she needed a reprieve from the past months of unrelenting stress. She looked thin and pale compared to last December when she felt carefree and vibrant, before the deployment had been announced. They left to head for their home leaving her for a much needed time out to recharge her batteries.

Four weeks had passed since Bunny had put in her plea for help on that bothersome kitchen faucet. Numerous phone calls just ended in frustration. The unit was based out of a city in the northern part of the state. Provisions had been made, and volunteers lined up to address the problems in that area only. Nothing had been put in place for the many families throughout the rest of the state. Requests to her location for any help had gone unanswered. No knight in shining armor would be charging in on a white horse to come to her aid. She could, however, apply for a one time emergency monetary dispensation to help cover the cost of the repair. She opted to forgo any further delays. She would take the matter into her own hands, she'd repair it herself.

She had borrowed books on drywall repair from the library to finish up some work in the house. Now, she would go in for plumbing information. The books made it sound too easy, and it was Mick that rode in to be her rescuer. On one of their visits to let grandma spoil Jack, Mick noticed the faucet still leaking.

"Mom, I'll be back tomorrow with my tools to fix this thing. I have repaired one before, but never totally replaced one. I am willing to try though. I'm sure together we can do it," he told her.

"Well, if we can't fix it at least the next guy that gets the job will earn his pay," she replied.

Sure enough, Mick showed up, with family in tow bright and early the next morning. They tore into the job like they knew what they were doing. It wasn't long before the old one had been ripped out. By referring to the instruction sheet and reference materials, they were able to complete the job in 45 minutes. After testing and retesting it, Mick was satisfied that they had successfully completed the plumbing job.

Bunny confessed to him over lunch that he had just saved her $130 plus mileage fees. She had checked with a plumber earlier. He had told her the job would take 2 hours at 65 buck an hour, that's the least he would have charged to do what Mick had just done.

"Well, mom they count in coffee breaks, and time to have a smoke or two in there you know," Mick joked.

October had indeed been a busy month. JW had finally gone overseas, the countdown clock had begun. Bunny had sent several packages to JW for much needed replacements parts on equipment he had taken with him. He did not have the luxury of going to a local store to purchase things he needed, there were no stores. The folks had moved back home. The last of the water problems had been put to rest she hoped. Emails continued to flow between JW and Bunny. Cards full of photos were sent to him to keep him updated on the grandbaby.

Bunny fell back into a routine. She got back to painting the remaining rooms downstairs. A paint job was needed on the hen house before bad weather set in, so Bunny began to tackle that next. She spent nearly a week scraping off old paint, and slapping on two coats of fresh, white paint. It was ready for the oncoming winter weather. Standing back to admire her handiwork she couldn't help but be proud of the job. With the hens parading around the yard, it looked like a beautiful oil painting hanging in a world famous art museum. She was more than satisfied with the results of her labor.

She managed to attend church and car club meetings regularly. It was in October that the members of Bunny's car club, The Central

Illinois Mustangers, began to send monthly care packages to JW and his brother. They were so generous that the entire unit would be able to share the bounty. Checks from the club had been presented to both JW, and his brother to purchase phone cards before they left. They would use them to stay in contact with home. JW had used his sparely to call Bunny, he wanted to save most of the time on the card for the upcoming holidays.

Leann wanted to get back to tutoring students on Saturdays starting in November. She had provided struggling students extra instruction from her home before Jack was born. She needed a babysitter to help out while she tended to her students. She couldn't care for Jack and teach at the same time. Bunny jumped on the chance to help, it gave her the perfect excuse to spoil baby Jack. The kids knew that, but allowed her to liberally spoil him anyway. She got out of the house for a full day while helping the kids out as well. On several occasions she had volunteered to stay over night when the baby was fussy to keep from going home to the big empty house. Readily, the kids had permitted her to stay. They had kept her from going totally crazy the past few months.

JW was on 12-hour duty shifts 6 days a week. He rarely put in only 12 hours since something was always calling him back to his duty station. The day off, if he actually got one was usually used to try to catch up on missed sleep, or to turn in laundry. Seldom did he really have a full day without work of some kind.

He managed to send a few email photos to her. They showed him in full gear standing in the hot sun in the middle of the barren desert. He was tired from the grueling schedule, and the heat of the desert he hadn't become accustomed to yet. Her heart ached to see him in such a desolate place, far from home and family. She just wanted to hold him, if even for a moment.

An email from him confirmed that the package Bunny had carefully packed for him filled with goodies from home had finally reached him. She had sent him a package with his favorite home made cookies, dried apple slices from their small orchard, and a few store bought snacks. He told her how much the items had meant to him including that the "cookie crumbs" tasted delicious.

He emailed a photo of himself standing in front of an armored vehicle with one of the Central Illinois Mustangers Club pennants flying from it, comically stating that he had found his Iraq Mustang. The club was going to love this picture. He tried to keep the mood of his emails to her as light as possible, knowing fully well that she was concerned about his welfare. He wouldn't have her worry about his routine or his safety.

In one of his emails, he told how he met the Post Commander. JW was rushing out of a building, swinging the door open hitting the Colonel in the back with the doorknob. The Colonel told him that he might have to press battery charges for the incident. JW stood there quivering looking for something to say.

"Great, Sir, does that mean I can go home?" he recovered quickly. They had a good, hearty laugh, and lengthy discussion after the awkward meeting.

The church honored all veterans the during November's second Sunday's service. She was called up to accept a certificate on his behalf as the large screen behind the pulpit displayed his picture. She received it with a white carnation tied with a red, white, and blue ribbon. As the line of veterans stretched across the front of the church, she was aware of the sacrifices all these men and women had made for their country. Awareness of the sacrifices made by their families also crossed her mind. She stood reverently with the brave service personnel that had already served their country proudly.

In mid November it was time to send off Christmas gifts to JW. Thanksgiving hadn't arrived yet, and she was forced to think of Christmas already. What was she to send?

"Bea, I need your help. I have an unconventional gift to send to JW. I need to know if he will think I'm nuts for mailing it to him. I plan on sending him a box filled with pinecones from our trees. Is that crazy?" Bunny needed to know.

"A little weird, but under the circumstances send it. Besides, everybody already knows you are off your rocker," Bea teased.

"Thanks, it's always nice to be a confirmed nut case by your friends," Bunny replied. With misgivings she mailed the package anyway.

Bunny was able to help Mick and Leann with some household repairs. Their back door needed to be replaced before winter. They wanted to add a storm door for extra insulation also. The weather had been unseasonably mild so far. Mick wanted to get the doors replaced before their luck ran out. He would not be able to install it without help, so Bunny assisted them. Leann and Bunny took turns helping him, and watching Jack, depending on the work that had to be done.

Mick had never replaced a complete door before, but Bunny had helped her father. She knew the basics of the process. Mick began tearing out the existing door to find it firmly stuck in place, try as he may the door would not budge from the frame.

He picked up a pry bar and hammer, "This calls for the JW method of home repairs. If it doesn't work beat it into submission."

With that he hammered away at the wooden frame, and pulled the door free leaving a huge gapping hole in the wall. They were ready to begin the next phase of the task. Installation started by laying the instruction sheet on the door. They all prayed for help in getting the job done. Together they were able to decipher the mysteries of the installation insert. Leann, Mick, and Bunny finished the job installing the steel entry door on the first day. Adding shims, caulking, and insulation around the frame Mick insured the door would be level and airtight.

"Well, mom we did it. I don't think a professional carpenter could have done a better job," Mick announce proudly as they stood back to admire their job.

"I am so proud of all of us. I think we just might make it through this thing together," Bunny said.

Leann dished out large pieces of pepperoni pizza for them while they gathered up tools. They visited for a few moments before Mick had to prepare to go to work his night shift. Bunny told them she would return the next day to help with the storm door before leaving for home.

The second day they tackled the storm door. Leann had to assist Mick more then because it required more lifting than Bunny could handle. A gentle rain began to fall the second day into the project. Poor Mick and Leann finished the job in the rain while Jack was put in Bunny's care. The job was finished just before the temperatures fell. A light snow began to fall as they gathered tools to come inside, but both doors were in place. They would be ready for the cold that was coming with the soft, white flakes.

Bea would not take no for an answer when she asked Bunny to Thanksgiving dinner at her mother-in-law, Betty's home. Bunny had known Betty for almost as long as she had known Bea. On more than one occasion when Bunny didn't feel like spending a night alone she had stayed with Betty. One night during a series of bad thunderstorms, Bunny had asked Betty if she could come in to weather the storms out together. Betty was a kind and caring person, always thinking of everyone else gladly agreed. They spent most of the night eating popcorn, and watching old movies on TV into the wee hours of the night. They joked with the rest of Betty's family about the slumber parties they both enjoyed so much.

A phone call from JW early on Thanksgiving morning lifted her spirits. They got to talk for 15 minutes. Oh, how wonderful he sounded. She had forgotten how much she loved to hear his laughter, it made her spirits soar. She was able to attend the dinner, and took photos of everyone acting slightly crazy to send to JW. They kept her there until 9pm so she wouldn't have to spend a lot of time alone.

A huge plate piled high with all the food from dinner was sent home with her to keep her eating. Everyone worried about her dropping weight. They made sure to encourage her to eat. She had lost a few pounds, but not enough to become overly concerned about. Their friends had promised JW he wouldn't be coming home to a skeleton.

The food she carted home that evening was proof that they intended to keep that promise.

A quick check of the email account had photos of JW and his brother enjoying a turkey dinner. They had been able to eat a holiday meal together. Bunny was glad they had each other. The pictures showed that the Army had done a great job of trying to make a good meal for the troops. That eased her mind as she slipped into bed that evening.

The weather had turned off cold quickly. Unseasonably warm temperatures gave way to the cold blast of winter. Bunny decided to make Goldie an inside dog. She had done her job well for the past five years as a guard dog keeping a diligent watch over the six acres she claimed as her own. It would be easier on both of them since she wouldn't have to make the trip out to the kennel twice a day in the cold and snow, the poor dog wouldn't have to bear the cold temperatures and winter winds. She would bring extra company and comfort for Bunny this winter as well.

Goldie had been brought into the garage, sometimes into the kitchen on extremely cold nights in the past. She had always enjoyed being near Bunny inside the warmth of the house. The task at hand now was to have Larkin accept her as one of the family. It was Larkin's house that this intruder was going to be invading. On a previous trip into her domain, Larkin had expressed her dislike of the dog by jumping on her and sinking all of her razor sharp, front claws into the dog's tender nose. Since that meeting the two of them had been kept apart, and the cat had been de-clawed.

The first thing that had to be done was to bathe Goldie to rid her of the outdoor dog smell. Larkin was confined to a room while the process of making Goldie ready to move inside proceeded. She was brushed, lathered up twice, rinsed, and a hair dryer used to complete the job. The little, golden colored dog hated water even though she was part lab. A lot of praise combined with special treats proved to her that a bath wasn't that bad, now she looked and smelled like an inside pup.

Larkin was set free to meet Goldie as a new member of the household. Immediately upon seeing the cat, she laid down on the floor covering her nose with both paws. She hadn't forgotten their first encounter. The dog lay motionless in the middle of the floor as Larkin slowly walked around her while the dog refused to move a muscle. Only her eyes moved following the cat. The cat reached out to poke her with a paw, and then turned to strut off. It was as if Larkin was flexing her authority saying," You can stay but I'm the boss around here." It had gone much better than Bunny hoped it would, at least there was no blood shed during this meeting.

It turned out to be a very good call on Bunny's part. December 1st brought an ice storm that knocked out power across the entire state, in fact several states suffered. It started out with snow that turned into freezing rain. Everything was covered in ice ½ inch thick with snow under it.

Bunny experienced a power outage early on the first night of the storm. Living in a rural area they were always prepared for the worst. JW made sure she had everything she would need to weather a storm like this. She had batteries, flashlights, a weather radio, and even a small battery operated TV to keep in contact with the outside world. There was 800 gallons of propane in the tank to run the gas fireplace to keep warm.

Knowing well in advance that the storm was headed her way, she had stocked up on groceries the day before it hit. Large containers filled with water lined the kitchen counters, because if the power went out the pump wouldn't work, and there would be no water to drink. She had 10 gallons stored in the basement, but since they had predicted this to be a large storm she preferred to be over prepared. She had her critters welfare as well as her own to think about, water was a necessity.

Even the hen house had been made ready to wait out the storm. She had turned on the water heater, filled the tank, and feeder in case she wouldn't be able to get to the hen house for several days. Extra layers of plastic insulated the window to add protection from the constant prairie winds. She had done all she could. It would have to be enough. Upstairs bedrooms were closed off leaving only the bathroom doors open. She really didn't want water lines to freeze and break. The fireplace was lit to keep the house warm enough to be livable. Extra layers of clothing were added to keep warm. She settled into the bed that still occupied the living room from her parent's stay for the night ahead.

The phones still worked for now, that was a miracle in itself. Her cell phone had been fully charged in preparation of the outage, so she would be able to call for help if the hard line phone went out. Everyone called to check on her. Mick and Leann still had power for the moment, and they begged her to come to their home. Bea wanted her to come in so she could keep and eye on her, others called to make sure she was safe.

Bunny decided to stay put. She would not try to travel the hazardous country roads. At home she was safe, which was better than stuck in a ditch freezing. It turned out to be a good call.

Power was restored to her home after only six hours. She was able to venture outside to take a few snapshots of the winter wonderland the next morning to send to JW. He had heard about the storm, which made him worry about her safety. She assured him that everything at home was up and running.

She was one of the luck ones, her home had been spared, others in the state had not been as fortunate. It took as long as two weeks to return power to some homes in a large city just 15 miles from her.

The ice and snow accumulation on the roof had to be about 6" thick. Once it began to melt, it slid off in massive sheets crashing to the ground. One chunk took shingles and two roof vents with it, allowing water to leak into the two upstairs bathrooms. Water issues yet again, maybe, she should just order wood to start building an arc.

Knowing that the problem had to be addressed, she quickly called a roofing company, and was added to their growing list of customers to have them come out for repairs. It would take weeks to just get an estimate. When she was finally able to get an estimate damages were going to cost her $425. Once again the cost was under the deductible for an insurance claim, this would be another unexpected expense. She was added to a growing waiting list for repairs to be made.

All in all, she was lucky. Some of her friends in town had a tree fall on their home. It had taken out the front part of their house making it unlivable for months. The repairs totaled $18,000 in all. Other friends had lost the entire contents of their packed refrigerators and freezers, costing them hundreds of dollars to replenish. Her problems seemed small when she compared them to others around her. God had blessed her with His mercy.

In a week the snow and ice had all but disappeared. A few flurries hung around just to remind her that winter was still there, but the roads were kept clear for travel. She kept busy with her routine of babysitting Jack and keeping an eye on her folks.

She wasn't in a festive mood by any means. It would have suited her just fine to cover up in bed to wait for the holidays to pass. She knew that was not an option, so she just put her best face forward and marched on.

Their large Christmas tree had been donated to the Armory for the previous year's party. Bunny thought that since she had no tree, she wouldn't have to go through the agony of putting one up. JW shamed her into purchasing a tree for Jack's first Christmas. Once the decorations were on the tree, and the lights started twinkling, she missed him even more. No gifts were placed under the tree; she delivered them as soon as they were wrapped. The only items she placed under the tree were a pair of combat boots and a helmet.

While she was trying to cope with all the holiday joy, plastering a smile on her face every day, her beloved "Pony" began to have problems. Earlier in the fall she had to take it into the dealership to have work done on the trunk. Either the trunk refused to open, or refused to close. It usually happened during shopping trips. Bunny found it difficult to look 'cool' driving the bright, yellow Mustang with toilet paper visible from the back window. Not only had that problem reoccurred, the battery was dead.

After charging it up and driving to the dealership, they told her that she had let it sit idle too long. A test on the battery showed it to be in good working order. The car alarm had simply drained the battery. They replaced parts on the trunk closure for the third time before sending her on her way.

She purchased a trickle charger to keep the battery up when she stored it for weeks on end. When she wasn't planning on taking it out, it was on the charger. It got plenty of road time in the days to come. She attended the Mustang club party, a church dinner, and went to open house parties. Christmas Eve she joined her in-laws for church service, dinner, and a drive through the local park to view Christmas light displays. She kept herself busy to the point of near exhaustion, but her mind was with him, her love, JW.

JW had sent her an email early in the month thanking her for the Christmas cookies, dried fruit, and photos she had mailed to him. Another box filled with pinecones had gotten there, too. Her crazy gift had been well received. He loved the fact that she had thought to send him pinecones from his very own trees. It made the place seem more like Christmas, it smelled like Christmas in the middle of the desert.

What made the gift so special was the fact that Bunny had an allergic reaction to anything with pine in it. If she brushed up against the trees when she was outdoors, a skin rash appeared. She had risked a good case of hives to send him this gift, and he knew it, that is what made this strange gift so dear to him.

Bunny began looking forward to Christmas Day when she got an exciting email from JW. He told her that he would be calling home to talk to her then. Mick, Leann, and Jack were coming for dinner, and the kids would get to talk to him also.

Two days before Christmas she got a call from him, this would be his Christmas call instead. He had volunteered for a mission so a

Soldier with small children could call home on Christmas Day. He had already emailed home, his children would be waiting for daddy's call. JW told him he would go on the mission in his place. It was a disappointment to know that the chance to talk to him on Christmas was not in the cards for her. She also understood that he put the needs of his troops above his own.

"I'm sorry Bunny, but he has little kids. They have had this video call set up for weeks. I can't let him go out and miss the kids on this special day," he told her.

"I understand. We can talk now. We don't need a special holiday to do that. I just need to hear your voice," she reassured him that he had made the right decision. She respected his thoughtfulness and his decision. Any call meant the world to her.

He had been able to pick up a few gifts for them from a bazaar he had visited. Hand carved wooden camels, wooden trinket boxes with mother of pearl inlays, and colorful rugs were sent home to share with the family. The most important piece in each box, the little notes he carefully tucked in meant just for her.

Much to her surprise, and everyone else's, he got back from where ever he had to go in time to call before Christmas dinner. The phone was passed around, and he chatted with everyone. He touched their hearts from across the miles of ocean water and desert sand.

Spirits remained high that day as they celebrated the birth of Christ. Later, he emailed a photo of himself and his brother having Christmas dinner. He was safe, and that was the greatest gift of all. She had spent the day with their handsome son and beautiful daughter-in-law. She was able to cuddle her darling grandson on his first Christmas. Joy filled her heart the entire day. It wasn't about trees or gifts; it was about the gift of love that God sent to the world, that's what she needed to remember. It was love that washed over her that holy day.

New Year's Eve was there sooner than Bunny wanted it to be. She was asked by friends and family to go to party after party. She declined all invitations to stay home. All she wanted to do was spend a quiet evening at home. She had given in to them for the entire month. Now, she wanted to be alone. She was fine, just in need of a little quiet time.

She went over a list in her head for her party plans; one lap cat, one faithful pup, Diet Coke, bag of chips, warm, fuzzy blanket, a big, fluffy pillow, and a stack of funny movies. She was ready to celebrate. Let the good times roll! She was asleep before 11 in front of the TV curled up with Goldie and Larkin.

CHAPTER FIVE

It was in early January that the doorbell broke. Replacing the batteries didn't solve the problem, so off to the local hardware store she went with the unit. She was almost on a first name basis with the clerks by now. They informed her that it was toast, the whole thing had to be replaced. The clerk helped her choose a new unit, and told her how to do the job. She was afraid of missing important packages or letters, so she installed it on that cold, snowy afternoon.

Two days later she came down with what she thought was a cold. She tried to fight it off as the snow mounted up in the drive. No way was she going to budge now. She would just hunker down to fight it off. A couple of days went by, and her cough got worse. She completely lost her voice, her chest hurt, and it was difficult to breathe. The only thing she could do was put the Jeep in four wheel drive, hoping to plow through the drifts to get to the clinic for help.

She didn't realize she was really sick until the nurse told her that her temperature was 103. She had x-rays taken that confirmed bronchitis along with her laryngitis. The doctor sent her home with a bag full of samples of medicines to take, and strict instructions to go to bed. The worst part of it all was that she was told not to talk for at least a week to rest her voice. She hoped JW would not try to call. Knowing that she was sick would just cause him stress that he didn't need.

Mick and Leann wanted her to come stay with them. No matter how much they pleaded for her to go with them she refused to take germs to her grandson. Leann checked on her frequently. She brought homemade soup and sandwiches to her. She made Bunny promise that if things got worse she would call them. Bunny jotted on a piece of paper, if someone calls you, and nobody is there it will be me.

Jackie offered to help with errands. She arrived with a bag of goodies after a few days to replenish her food supply. A visit from her helped Bunny's recovery as much, if not more, as the meds she had been prescribed.

Bunny was just content then to snuggle down under the covers for rest. Larkin and Goldie cuddled up next to her to keep watch over her. She began to feel better after three days on the medication. It would take several weeks to completely get her voice back, even longer for her to get rid of the cough that lingered.

After a week she decided to make a run to town for groceries and feed for the hens, the truck needed to be taken out for a run anyway. When she returned and unlocked the shed the door handle unit on the overhead door broke off in her hand. She really wasn't in the mood to deal with this now. She unloaded the feed and groceries, then slipped back into bed. The whole ordeal of shopping, then breaking the lock on the door to JW's workshop left her weak, tired, and frustrated.

Knowing that repairs to the lock was too big a job for her to tackle she turned to her church for help. The church members told her earlier that they would help with anything. They had called several times during the winter to check on her welfare, knowing that she was alone in the country. She asked if they could help repair the door. She needed to keep the shed locked since it held all JW's tools, truck, and lawn equipment, including the new tractor. Two church members came out to access the damage. They told her what needed to be done before leaving to get repair parts for the door.

The father and son team returned a few days later to replace the handle. Weather stripping on the bottom of the door was replaced to stop the water that had been leaking in, a bar for reinforcing the middle panel was added for support against the wind. Everything was adjusted and oiled by the time they finished. More than she had asked, or hoped for was done. They only thing they charged her for was the cost of the parts they had to purchase. It was God's love put into action.

Health and a stronger faith had been restored to her weary body. She was able to finish the month on a high note. The roofing company had completed repairs to the roof during a break in the weather, and she had started painting both upstairs baths.

JW emailed her that he would be coming home on leave sometime in March. She didn't want the stain from the leaking roof on the ceilings of the bathrooms to be visible for him to start asking questions about. All these problems would be kept secret for now.

The bath redecorating was completed with new themes. Since he had been used to the bland brown of the desert, she wanted a bright and cheerful color scheme. She painted the walls of his bath a light, cheery yellow. Three baskets of green, yellow, and red silk plants were arranged along one wall. The shower curtain was an ocean scene with colorful fish swimming in a coral reef. She chose new towels in bright red and blue to finish the look. It was warm and inviting.

The other bath was painted a light, coral shade. The shower curtain was white with thin lines of every bright color in the book. She repainted the shelves white, and hung pictures of orange with white flowers on the walls. Matching silk flowers were placed on the shelves and around the clock on the opposite wall. Teal rugs and towels completed the look. By the time she was done, it looked like it was ready to host a carnival. These projects had kept her busy while winter played out through the rest of that month.

JW emailed that sandstorms had been going through his part of the world at fairly regular intervals. He mentioned that he had been ill for a few days that month. Knowing that he rarely complained she could only assume that it had been worse than he told her. Neither one of them would confess to the other just how ill they had been.

A bright spot for him was a trip from a cattle rancher in Texas to their location. He had brought his own steaks to the unit for a very welcomed cookout. The troops had enjoyed a fresh steak dinner flown in from the states just for them. It was a relief from the daily chow. It also was proof of the support and generosity of some people back in the states.

The weather turned cold again bringing with it snow. February was a month of blizzards with below zero wind chills. She continued her routine, getting out to church, and babysitting until the roads were closed due to snow. During a 24hour period 15.8 inches of snow fell, which was blown around by 30 mph winds. Motorist caught off guard had to be rescued by snowmobiles from their stranded vehicles. Trying to travel was a nightmare, so she remained home ready to sit out another winter storm.

Bunny caught the flu bug again, and went to bed for rest. She just couldn't completely shake this thing. It would require more rest and medication. She needed to get a package in the mail for JW's upcoming birthday. If she failed to mail it soon, it wouldn't arrive in time. Leann shopped, wrapped, and mailed the box filled with granola bars, dried fruits, and little cakes. Thankfully, her help would keep him from ever knowing that Bunny had been ill. The kids and Jack also caught a cold; everyone was down for a time. Even JW emailed her saying he was feeling out of sorts again.

It was the day after Valentine's Day before the roads were clear enough to travel. She managed to shake off health problems long enough to get to town. Bea had something for her. JW had sent her a dozen lavender-colored roses, knowing that purple was her favorite color. He had gotten on the Internet to order them months in advance to be sure they would be ready on the 14th. He was so romantic, how could she help but love him?

By the 20th Jack had learned to sit up, just days before he turned

6 months old. Everyone was beginning to regain strength and return to normal. The temperatures reaching 50 by the end of the month helped. Snow was melting fast. Hopefully, spring was near. Rains helped to finish off the rest of snow as the ground turned into a soggy bog of mud.

Final plans for the upcoming leave were announced by email to Bunny. JW was coming home for 2 weeks sometime the end of March. The exact dates had not been given to him yet, but he was coming home. He would be home to celebrate their anniversary, and to spend a few brief days with them.

Bunny had to send JW another package before his leave, filled with items he needed. She rushed into town to mail the box before the post office closed. As she stood in line at the post office, she noticed everyone staring at her and backing away. She went about her business, and on the way to the car realized what they had been looking at. In her haste to get to town; she had forgotten to remove two eggs from her pockets that she had gathered before leaving home. The front of her pants were wet, broken eggshells in her pocket told the story. She stood in the parking lot at the dumpster flinging broken eggs into it laughing at her stupidity. Everyone in line must have thought she had wet her pants. To make matters worse, the leather seat in the Mustang was also covered in raw eggs, which she had to clean up. God did have a sense of humor, and today she needed a laugh.

The incident was reported at the next Mustang Club meeting. A monthly award was given out to unfortunate car owners caught doing stupid things involving their cars. Bunny was the proud owner of the Half-Fast Award for egging her own car…from the inside.

She had a lot to do to prepare for JW's leave. Bunny decided she needed to begin repairing, and replacing things that had fallen apart in the past few months. She bought a new flashlight to replace the one that she'd run over with the truck. She found one similar to his favorite one hoping he wouldn't notice the minor differences.

It took her one entire afternoon to repair the kitchen drawer that had broken. The whole drawer front had fallen off one day when she opened it. The bracket and track that held it in place broke, so everything had to be replaced and screwed back into place. It had been held up with duct tape for months, this had to be done because he was sure to notice that.

Two calculators had been dropped on the cement floor in the basement and shattered. New ones were purchased to replace them. JW's staple gun that she used to hang plastic in the hen house had broken. Thankfully, she found the exact same one. She made sure to get it good and dirty, so he wouldn't be able to tell it from the old one.

The only thing she couldn't repair was the tree trimmer she broke while trimming the apple trees last fall. She had no idea how to put it back together. The shingles on the roof that constantly flapped in the wind were beyond her control also. Those two things would have to go unattended.

An early March storm dumped 3 more inches of snow on them. By the 10th of the month the temperature reached 60, and it was gone. The rest of the month continued to have mild even warm weather with highs of 75. It was a perfect time to get ready for his homecoming.

Bea was having problems with her knee. Bunny took her in for shots several times to see if they could relieve the pain. Hopefully, with shots, and rest the doctor could postpone knee replacement surgery for a while. She had to tend to her friend to help her recover.

Jack was in full swing of teething. He was fussy, and running a slight temp. Poor Leann was ready to pull her hair out when Bunny asked if she could help. A couple of nights during the month she stayed all night with them. They worked like a wrestling tag team to ease his pain and restlessness. First one, then the other would rock him, walk the floor, and try to get him to sleep. They fed him, burped him, and sang silly songs to him. They did anything, and everything, to help ease his discomfort. Even Bunny's Little Green Frog song didn't work. The frog song always put him to sleep until now.

During the month he also learned to crawl. Grandma spent hours with him teaching him to say "bye-bye" while waving his little hand. He added that to the one word he had already picked up, "hi." He was learning new things all the time.

Just before St Patrick's Day, Leann and Mick came over to celebrate Bunny's birthday. Leann had baked a cake for her. Mick and Leann prepared lunch while grandma got to play with Jack. They gave her a huge, scented candle that Bunny never would splurge, and spend the money to buy for herself. JW had sent her a wooden jewelry box and a brass vase. It was a wonderful birthday spent with her family. The only thing missing was JW.

Time seemed to drag, even though she tried to keep herself occupied. She attended a baby shower, had lunch several times with her in-laws, and even attended the Mustang Club St Patrick's Day dinner. She had gone to the annual corned beef and cabbage dinner Bea's family held at Betty's house. As busy as she was, her heart and mind were always with JW.

A band had come to JW's location to put on a concert for the troops. His youngest brother had sent him a package including a set of oversized, green, shamrock shaped, sunglasses. He included a box of Lucky Charms cereal and sparkling, green beaded, necklaces to complete the look. Everyone had to get their picture taken wearing his glasses and beads, while holding the cereal. They needed a bit of comic relief now and then.

Bunny found a beautiful sunny day to clean and shampoo the carpets downstairs. While she had the machine out, she cleaned the interior on the Jeep and Mustang as well. They were both washed and waxed. She would do anything at this point to keep busy. Everything had to be as perfect as possible for JW. The warm weather encouraged the grass to grow tall and green. It was going to have to be mowed, or he would do it during his leave. She wanted him to relax on leave not work.

Bunny mowed with the trimming tractor, then took the larger one out to finish the rest. While mowing near the back that gently slopped into a grove of willows, the mower got stuck in mud. A field tile had broken, before she knew it, she was stuck. The tractor had 4wheel drive, so she used that to try to pull free. Try as she may, it didn't help to move the tractor out. It just sank in deeper.

She took the freshly shined and polished Jeep to pull the tractor out. The Jeep became stuck too, in spite of the 4wheel drive on it. Now what was she to do?

"Mick, it's mom. I have done something stupid. I have the John Deere tractor and the Jeep stuck in the 'back forty'," she called her son for advice.

He instructed her on how to work out the problem. He would come to help, but his shift started in 15 minutes. With his instructions she managed to get the Jeep out of the mud, but the tractor remained bogged in the mire. Leann and Jack drove up as she was pacing the yard, searching for a solution. She could not leave the expensive, new tractor out all night with rain on the way.

"I'll call the church. Maybe someone out this way has a truck, or tractor that can pull you out," Leann suggested as she began making phone calls.

It was 4 pm by then, almost everyone was at work, or in the fields, too busy to help until morning. What was Bunny to do? Bunny decided to call for a tow truck. After 4 calls to various companies, all refusing to tackle the job because of the location, Bunny and Leann prayed. 'God please help us get the tractor out and back to the shed.'

The next call started out much the same as the others, but ended by the receptionist giving her a phone number of a tow company that owned a four wheel drive tow truck. He may attempt the task.

Bunny was on it like a duck on a June bug. He was on his way home, just a few miles from her location. He'd come and at least look into the situation. He agreed to try, if she didn't mind the ruts he would probably leave in the area. Mind? As long as the tractor would be rescued from the muddy pit she would deal with that later.

He carefully positioned his truck into place and pulled her free. She started the tractor for fear that she had trashed it. JW's new tractor had to be undamaged. It had to be. Fortunately, for her the tow truck owner used to run a lawn service. After a quick inspection of the tractor, he was able to informed her it was in proper working order, but very muddy.

Just to make sure, Bunny called the salesman that had sold them the tractor. He was just coming back from a vacation. He agreed to stop by on his way home to checked it over. He helped her wash the mud off everything, and then took it for a test drive. He also confirmed that it was in tip-top shape, except for the light that had fallen off last summer. He promised to order a new one to replace it before JW's return. The soft mud yielded to the tractor allowing it to get stuck but caused no damage. Thank God, he provided two caring professionals to come to her aid, protected the new tractor, and sent her Leann for comfort.

Before JW arrived home on leave, she would fill in the ruts with dirt from other areas on the property using the end loader. The bare earth would be covered with old straw. She would just have to keep him away from that side of the yard. If asked, she could always tell him it was a landscaping project gone wrong. Which, would in reality be totally true. It had to do with landscaping, and there was no doubt that it had gone terribly wrong.

Word came through that JW had been moved to the slot of the Unit Detachment Commander. He sent home a disc of pictures for her with a program of the ceremony for the scrapbook she would be making. She was so very proud of him.

The night before she was to meet him at the airport, he called her from Scotland. At 11:30 pm she heard his voice announce that he was on his way home to her. In a few short hours she would be holding him in her arms. Finally, he was going to be home for the anticipated leave.

She barely slept the night before his arrival. Tossing and turning, trying to sleep she was certain that she had worn out a set of sheets in the process. Giving in finally, she got up at 4am. Wired for his arrival she finished a few last chores and got ready to meet Bea at 1:30 pm in town.

A small welcome home party had gathered at the airport to greet JW. Bea and Jean were there with a bunch of balloons. Mick and Leann brought Jack for long awaited meeting with his grandpa. Jack was dressed in a camouflage T-shirt and pants with a little tan, boonie hat. And, Bunny was there.

The flight in had been delayed for several hours. A loudspeaker announcement that the plane had landed brought a cheer from their small group. The passengers filed through the gate into the airport one by one until a uniformed Soldier came in. JW was there.

Bunny raced to him and held him repeating over and over, "You are here. You are finally home."

Mick and Leann in turn hugged him, then introduced him to the grandson he was meeting for the first time. At seven months old no one knew what to expect from Jack. Bunny constantly showed him pictures of grandpa, but she wasn't sure that it would trigger anything when they met face to face. Jack looked at him for a moment then reached out to put a little hand on each side of his grandfather's face, and smiled. It was as if he was saying, "Hi grandpa."

Bea and Jean who had been snapping photos came up to hug the returning Soldier. The balloons were presented to him. He was glad to be back, and proud of the reception he received. After a few minutes of visiting, they escorted him to the car to go home, a place he had left nine months and many miles ago.

On the way to the parking lot, he stopped to pick a dandelion from the grass, "I had no idea how beautiful these things really were. I've been fighting to keep them out of the yard for years. Now they look so different to me."

He was astonished at the green grass and the spring flowers in bloom. He noticed the smallest details of changes the town had undergone in the months he had been away. As the car pulled into the drive, he commented to Bunny how beautiful the place looked. It was just as he remembered it. If he only knew the trials that had been overcome to make it look that way. She just smiled, happy that she was able to impress him. She was happy that she had been able to hold everything together, up to this point, anyway.

He was greeted by happy, little critters wanting attention. Luggage was left on the floor near the back door, he walked from room to room glad to be in his own home. He approved of the redecorating job that had taken place. The living room walls had been changed from a pink blush to a medium tan with room accessories in burgundy to match the new drapes.

The kitchen and dining room were a warm yellow instead of the off white. One wall in the dining room with an area around the kitchen cabinets was now a medium blue. Drapes in the dining room were a tweed material of brown, yellow, orange, and blue. It gave the room a welcoming atmosphere. He was pleased with the changes, and happy to be home.

JW wanted a shower and hot food. Bunny sent him to hit the shower while she threw a frozen pizza in to bake. He took a long hot shower. Usually, he was limited on time in the showers, three to five minutes, so to be able to take a twenty-minute shower was heaven to him. He dressed in jeans and a long sleeve shirt, his first civilian clothes in months. He was met downstairs with huge slices of pizza, and an endless glass of iced tea. They sat in the living room on the couch, gobbling up the whole pizza, and talking.

He looked so very tired. Complaining of a headache, and his ears being stopped up, he brushed it off to all the traveling. Bunny was concerned about him though. She planned on keeping him at home to allow him to rest for the first 3 days of leave. Everyone wanted to visit, but he needed to rest. She needed him all to herself for now.

On the second full day home, he still had the headache. By this time he couldn't hear at all on one side. Bunny talked him into going to the clinic to be checked over. She was glad they went because he had a sinus infection. Part of the problem with his hearing was due to the change in air pressure on the plane rides over. The doctor told him that it would clear up on it's own in 5 to 7 days. At least Bunny was relieved knowing he had medicine for the sinus infection, and no ear infection was found.

They celebrated their anniversary at home a few days later. Neither one of them felt the need to go out to a fancy restaurant. Bunny prepared a home cooked meal instead. They could enjoy dining at home in peace and quiet without a crowd.

Mick, Leann, and Jack came over as much as they could. JW was thrilled to spend time with Jack. They wrestled on the floor, played with blocks, and stuffed toys. Jack loved the attention from his grandpa. JW was in awe at how happy Jack was all the time. He was full of energy, and brought them so much joy.

They had JW's folks, Donna and John, over one afternoon. They met Bea, Slick, and Jean for Chinese food. The Central Illinois Mustangers Club threw a potluck dinner for him at a local VFW hall. He got plenty of food and fellowship.

They decided to go visit Bunny's folks. Now, she had to break the news to JW about mom before he saw the frail little woman that her mother had become. She had sent photos to him the past several months, but was always careful to disguise mom's appearance. Bunny would put her mom behind other people to shield her thin frame from the camera. She would have her wear a bulky sweater, or make sure the angle of the shot made her look heavier than the poor woman was. There would be no hiding the thin body from him in person. Besides, he was sure to pick up on the confusion the poor woman couldn't shake.

"There is something I need to tell you before we visit the folks," Bunny started the dreaded confession.

"What is it Bunny? Is there something wrong?" JW knew there was because of the tone in her voice.

"Before I came out to see you the last time in September, mom had a heart attack, it was a major heart attack. She's been very ill. She's not like she used to be. Because of the heart problem she is confused sometimes," Bunny swallowed hard trying to choose the right words, "You are going to see a big change in her. I just didn't want you walking in there not knowing about this."

"Exactly when did this happen?" he asked her.

"It was early on the morning of September 11th. That's why they stayed with me after I came back from you seeing you. She was in the hospital the whole time I was visiting you. I just didn't want you to worry about her or me. That's why I haven't told you until now. But, you have to know now. You have to be prepared when you see her," Bunny hoped that he wouldn't be angry for her silence up to this point in time.

He drew her close to him and held her, "Bunny you are so strong. I love you."

With all that said, they took off for the long awaited visit. Mom was having a fairly good day, her confusion was minimal. JW watched her closely. Bunny could tell he was able to pick up the differences in her appetite and speech.

"I look just awful," Mom confessed, "I've been a little sick. But, I'm better now."

"You have to be well to welcome me home when this is over, so don't go getting sick on them again," JW told her.

"I'll try," the poor woman said.

"No, you can't try. You have to promise me you'll eat, get strong, and be here to dance at my welcome home party when I get back," JW replied.

She shook her head, and uttered the words, "I promise."

They had a wonderful visit telling old stories and laughing. The past was easier for her to remember at times than the present. And, all too soon it was time to leave.

"Remember your promise," JW reminded her as he stepped into the car.

She nodded waving as the car drove away. Bunny hoped that the visit had given her mom renewed strength.

Easter arrived while he was on leave. They went to church service, and back home to a ham dinner in the cozy dining room. It was just the two of them. They enjoyed the day together, knowing that the following Saturday he would have to leave for the desert, back to the war.

Unfortunately, for her, JW stumbled upon the area in the yard she was trying to keep him from finding. He had taken the dog out for a walk while she was in the shower. He continued questioning her until she confessed the entire story to him. She related the whole thing, including the tow truck incident. He vowed to show her how to get the Ford tractor started, so she could at least use that to pull out stranded vehicles in case it happened again.

He realized the reason that she hadn't been able to get the old Ford running for months. It was the starter. It had gone out on the old tractor. Working on worn-out equipment was the last thing she wanted him to do on leave since he had recently been ill. But, he wanted to do the repair job for his peace of mind giving her another resource to have on hand.

He took the starter to a shop, and had them rebuild it quickly, so he could reinstall it. Removing it was the easy part. Trying to put everything back in place was difficult in the limited space allowed for the piece to slip back into the correct position.

Bunny tried to help by holding a light for him to get the piece into place. After several attempts she couldn't help herself and offered a suggestion.

"Why don't we stop to pray to ask God for his help? It worked when we replaced Mick's door, and again when I had the tractor stuck," Bunny told JW.

"I don't have the time to stop to pray right now. I have to get this thing put back together," he stated continuing to work the piece into place.

It just refused to line up. After two hours of wrestling with the starter JW laid it down, looked toward the rafters in the workshop and said, "God, help me!"

He picked up the starter to guide it into place. It fell into the empty space as soon as he began to put it back into position. After tightening it down, he looked up to see Bunny smiling down at him.

"I know you don't have to say it. But, if God knew I needed help why didn't He just help me fix it?" he asked her.

"He knew you needed help. God was just waiting for you to ask for it. When you did He gave you the help you needed. He just wanted you to ask him," Bunny explained.

"Got it. I had to ask first," He grabbed her hand and held it. "Thanks for your help, my love."

Later that week they were walking the dog in the evening sharing the glow of a glorious sunset. He commented on how happy he was that Bunny had been able to keep up the yard and household. She had not told him of the problems she had over come to keep things running smoothly. She was happy that he thought she was doing a good job at maintaining things. As they were standing in the front yard admiring the last of the sun's rays casting shadows over the green grass, a shingle blew off the roof landing at their feet.

"Well, I guess I need to tell you we have a few loose, flapping shingles up there," Bunny smiled as she admitted to the roofing problem.

"I'll get them tomorrow. I know you can't do that. It shouldn't take long. Anything else I need to address before the week is out?" he asked.

"No, I think you found everything I hid that was broken and fixed it," Bunny laughed.

They walked hand in hand into the house to plan the rest of the week. His leave was coming to an end soon.

Saturday morning arrived bringing with it rain. The day was as dark as her spirits. They rose early, so Bunny could take him to the airport to drop him off for the long trip back to rejoin his unit. On the drive in, they decided that they wouldn't drag out his departure.

She walked him inside, gave him a hug, and kissed him. She tried to be brave, but the tears told the story of her heart. JW returned the kiss, then he turned to head to the check in area while she walked away from him in silence. She sat for a few minutes in the parked car as the rain danced off windshield thinking how empty she felt once again. She was going back home, back to a life without him for a few more months before his final return home. Just a few more months then he would be home for real.

It was only after his return to the unit that Bunny learned from Tracey that he almost missed his leave. He had been ill just a couple of days before his departure. He had passed out after complaining of not feeling well. After the medics attended to him, it was questionable if they would clear him for travel to come home. He had been in the hospital the evening before he was to depart, but he bounced back, making it home to Bunny. He never told her during his leave about this incident. He knew she would worry even more. And, she never confided in him that she knew of this episode.

CHAPTER SIX

Things got back into what had become a normal rhythm for her. Bunny resumed her usual routine. She tried to stay busy for sanity's sake.

One morning she went to help a bunch of volunteers sew neck coolers to send in care packages to the troops. When asked why she was there, Bunny told them about JW and his brother. She just wanted to help the troops anyway she could. Before she left later that afternoon, they gave her a box with enough neck coolers to supply two of them to each of the Soldiers in JW's unit. After soaking the strips in water, they were put around the neck to cool the Soldiers down in the heat of the burning desert sun. Summer was on the way with 120 to 130 degree heat. They would really need them.

Many of the men and women working that day had seen war before. They knew how much things like this meant to a Soldier away from home. What a blessing these hard working caring people were to their country. What a blessing they were to Bunny, and the Soldiers that would be receiving these gifts. She hugged each one of them, thanking them for their gift of time and talents. She dropped off the package in the mail on her way home knowing that they would be put to use as soon as the box was opened.

Jack had three teeth by the end of April. He was grandma's pride and joy. When she was just about at the end of her rope, Bunny could count on baby Jack to fill her heart with joy. Spending time with Mick, Leann, and Jack always inspired her, and they kept her on track with encouragement and love. They continued to bring her peace even in the troubled times she faced through their faith and hope. They became a fountain of love, always available to her.

After Bunny realized that she had successfully broken the tank sprayer on the trimming tractor, she bought a small hand held sprayer to zap weeds. Mick and Dad had both looked at the unit to try to fix it. It was concluded that the motor was probably burned out. JW would have to install a new one, or rebuild the old one if that was the case. For the time being, she would let it go until his return. He could do whatever he wanted to with the thing. Right now she wanted to burn it.

She assembled all the supplies she needed to spray weeds. It was only going to be a small area in the front of the house. There was no way she would be able to keep up the entire property. Spraying the few weeds she had in the grass would not be a problem. It would at least keep them under control until fall. The weed killer was prepared in the tank, and she began to spray.

On the second trip through the grass, Bunny sprayed a ground nest of wasps or hornets. Whatever they were, they were mad. She ended up flinging the sprayer on the ground, running into the back yard, hoping they wouldn't follow. She found out that day that she wasn't allergic to bee stings since they managed to sting her over 25 times before she was free and clear of them.

Her face and upper body suffered most of the stings that ended up leaving large red swollen spots the size of quarters. One or more of the little devils had gotten under her shirt and left the worst of the wounds there. The weeds would be left alone to grow as they pleased after that. Before it was time to mow the grass again, Eugene informed her on how to locate the nest of stinging insects. He told her how to get rid of them, so a repeat performance would not occur while mowing. Bunny did as instructed to put an end to their rule of terror in the front yard. Carefully, she mowed the grass in the area of the attack, ever watchful for any sign of the swarm to reappear. She had managed to kill them off, or they had found a better place to set up housekeeping. Happy with the absence of the pests she mowed along. The area along the back where the John Deere tractor had gotten stuck was a bit wet, so she mowed there with the trimming tractor. Almost finished with the entire yard she heard a loud pop. The tractor slowed to a full stop. The motor was still running, but it wasn't moving.

"What now," was all she could think? With great apprehension she turned to look behind her. Not only did she have a flat tire on the right rear, it had blown off the rim. Once again, she was in the 'back forty' with a disabled tractor. After removing her ear protection and cap, she threw her head back to laugh. It wasn't funny. It was hilarious! Maybe she had just learned to accept the trauma of the day, or maybe she had finally turned that corner from partially sane to total insanity?

"Hey, Mick, it's mom. I got a flat tire on the little tractor way out back. Can you help me get her up to the shed?" Bunny laughed when she called her son.

"I'm on my way mom," was all Mick said. Within ten minutes he was by her side to help.

Together they used the old Ford with a large chain to pull it to the shed. Mick tried getting the tire reseated on the rim, but it was not to be. Bunny thanked her son. They both laughed at how things just kept falling apart.

She would just stop to deal with it later. It just wasn't worth the emotional capital she would have to spend in order to deal with the matter right now. Her emotional bank account was running very low today.

It had become a running joke between Tracey and Bunny, every Friday evening they talked to each other to compare notes on their week. They had to see who had the worst luck for the past 7 days in a row. Bunny usually won the contest hands down although Tracey ran a close second. Some weeks it was a tie game. Laughing at each others misfortunes helped to put them into perspective anyway. Knowing someone else had rotten luck made one feel better for some odd reason.

Mom had not been feeling well since early April. Several trips to the doctor didn't help with the nausea, and occasional vomiting she had experienced for a month. On May 2nd Bunny called to find her too ill to keep her medications down. Mom refused to go to the hospital until Bunny insisted dad bring her in. It was either that, or Bunny would personally come down, hog tie her, and do it. She finally agreed to come in on her own. Bunny met them in the emergency room. Her appetite had fallen off, and she looked thinner than ever. She weighed only 87 lbs. Bunny regretted letting them leave to live on their own. She felt responsible for her mother's condition.

Mom was admitted to the hospital for tests. The final outcome of which showed that she had several infections. She had a urinary tract infection, pneumonia, and a serious infection in her colon. All of them masked by the pain medications she took for a ruptured disc in her lower back with several cracked vertebrae. The pain medicine had not allowed her to feel the pain from the other problems until they were totally out of control.

Immediately, the doctors ordered two antibiotics to attack the infections. Mom was confused and disoriented from the pain, vomiting, and drugs. Bunny refused to leave her in the hospital alone. She quickly set up a cot near her bed to stay the night. She sent her weary father home with a family member to care for him.

The family was called to her beside once again. They would take the day shift. Bunny would be there at night to make sure she got the best of care at any hour. The hospital staff welcomed the family to stay. As soon as her brothers or dad came in for the day shift, Bunny left for a few hours of sleep. She needed to check the critters and pick up mail. After a hot shower with a change of clothes, she was off to the hospital for her shift every evening. She packed her meals, so she wouldn't have to leave her mother's bedside.

One night during the wee hours of the morning, mom suffered another heart episode, as the doctor called it. No further serious damage had been done to her heart, but she was continuing to get weaker. She became unable to eat without vomiting afterwards, the sight of food made her nausea return.

The grim truth came down to the family from the doctors on their morning rounds, mom wasn't getting better. There was nothing else they could do. Medicare was going to have to discharge her soon. They suggested a nursing home for her to spend her last few days in. Basically, they were sending her away to die! Dad and Bunny refused to allow her to go to a nursing home to die.

Bunny stepped out of her room early the next morning while mom slept. She called Bea to give her an update. Shamelessly, she wept finding comfort from her friend's prayers and words of hope. Bea sent her strength to do what she knew she must do. When dad came in for the day Bunny left in a rush to get home.

Bunny recently had Mick move the bed from the living room back to the guest bedroom. She knew that Mick was working, and that bed had to be moved back into the living room. She called on her church family for help. Bunny had just gotten home with her parents when two young men from the church arrived to move the furniture. Working quickly, they had everything in place within a matter of minutes.

The nursing staff and the doctors had informed Bunny and her dad what to expect when the end came. Her poor old heart was giving out. Her body would begin to shut down system by system. When her kidneys failed, she would slip into a coma, in a few days she would be gone.

How were they going to bear it? Bunny and her dad would just have to make her as comfortable as possible for as long as possible. They'd let God handle the details. It would be difficult at best, but she could not put her in a strange place to die. If she were to pass on into God's heavenly kingdom, she would do it at home. She would be with the people she loved.

It was on May 10th that mom was released, and taken to Bunny's house. They had given her all the antibiotics she needed, all the infections were gone. She was able to eat light snacks, and drink cans of Ensure, a meal substitute. Chuck told them if she got four containers of that down each day she would have 1500 calories daily. All the nutrition she would need was in those cans, eating anything else would just be added calories to help her gain back weight.

Dad and Bunny continued to care for her, welcoming the visiting nurses who checked on her. At first she slept almost all the time, only waking to drink her Ensure, or take medicines. After a few days she began getting out of bed to sit on the sofa for the morning TV programs.

By the end of that week, she started to sit with them at the dining room table to nibble on snacks, or meals Bunny prepared special for her. She even gave herself sponge baths, and dressed herself with a little assistance. She was gaining strength and weight. Could it be the doctors had been wrong? She appeared to be better…stronger.

The doctors had set up an appointment to see her a week after her release from the hospital. They were amazed that they actually showed up, let alone the fact that she had color in her cheeks, and had gained a few precious pounds back. Her doctor told her he really didn't think they'd make it this far.

After a quick exam, he proclaimed her to be on the mend. She was really getting better, no sign of infection, and her lungs were clear. They were instructed to take her home. They were to continue the tender loving care regiment. She wasn't out of the woods yet, but she wasn't knocking on death's door either.

Dad and Bunny felt relief as they pushed the wheel chair to the waiting car. They had made the right decision to work on her recovery at home instead of sending her away for others to care for her. God had indeed taken care of all the details. He wasn't ready to call this angel home yet, she still had work to do on earth.

Having a boost of confidence from the doctor's report, they threw themselves into her care with more resolve than before. They were determined to continue the progress she had made in that one week. As long as she was drinking the meal substitute Bunny allowed her to have anything she wanted to eat. If she ate something they were elated.

Ice cream bars were served for breakfasts; pudding was prepared for lunch, baked potato for a 10 pm snack wasn't a problem either. From the unconventional diet she gained strength and weight. The scales began to tip up slowly. She could do more for herself with each passing day. Bunny thanked God for this miracle.

Each day posed new challenges, but they were working as a team to overcome it all. Eugene and dad repaired the flat tire on the tractor during one of the hot May afternoons. It would be ready for use now. They made sure they had a good supply of the Ensure on hand at all times. Chuck had to return home, but called often to help them by phone to answer their questions. He was always available to them give any help he could.

Bunny and her father worked hard to keep things running smoothly. It seemed to help mom's confusion if things were kept on a strict schedule. They worked very hard to keep her fed, clean, and entertained.

The schedule was interrupted by a breakdown of the washing machine. It would not drain the water after the rinse cycle. Bunny had a large load of sheets and heavy towels soaking in water. After playing with the control knob, she finally tricked the thing into draining the tank, then on to spin the laundry.

She made a few phone calls to see about a quick repair. Each one of the shops told her it had to be the timer going out. Since the washer was 15 years old, it would be wiser to buy a new washer than to put the money into that one they informed her. The next morning as mom napped she went into town to purchase a new one.

She chose a shop where a church member worked for her

purchase. He made sure she got exactly what she needed. No fancy bells and whistles, just the bare bones machine was all she wanted. He personally set up delivery for it the next day. It was much easier than she had hoped it would be. She was able to return before mom woke up.

Her delivery was to be made in late afternoon, but by 6 pm it still had not arrived. She needed that thing in place and working. She was more than a bit short on the phone with the dispatcher. She was told that the driver was lost, and couldn't find his way to her home. Bunny told the gal on the phone to have the driver call her personally for directions. That was one problem with living in the country nobody could ever find you. After 7 the driver finally called, he was really lost by this time. She tried to find out where he was from the descriptions he gave her of his surroundings. She told him to stay put, she would come and find him, somehow.

"Look for a bright yellow car. When you see it start honking so I can find you, " Bunny told him.

Bunny gave dad instructions on mom's snack and meds in case she didn't return in time to give them to her. She grabbed the Mustang keys to fly to the spot where she hoped the truck would be waiting. He wasn't there. He could only be in one other place 6 miles away. She sped off in search of the lost washer.

He began honking as soon as she rounded a corner. Well, she had found him, now to get him to her house. She pulled up next to him. After instructing him to follow her home, they were off. He was a young guy about 20 looking beat from the day's work. She took the shortcut on the back roads to the house, since he had no idea where he was anyway, she could give him instructions on getting back to town later.

He apologized for the problems he had caused. Bunny assured him it was fine. They would soon be finished, and they could all call it a day. He was there now, she needed him to get the job done quickly with as little noise as possible. Within ½ hour he was leaving.

By that time mom was totally confused by the commotion of the installation. It was difficult to get her calmed down enough for the next round of pills. It took until 11 that evening to get her mother ready to go to bed. She kept insisting that it was morning, and they needed to get up for breakfast. This was positive proof that Bunny had to keep a rigid format for each day's activities.

The next morning mom had forgotten about the previous nights adventures. The new dawn brought a new day of hope. Dad was in need of a break, so Bunny sat him on the new tractor to mow. He needed a break from the household chores he had been doing. Bunny could handle things inside for today.

Dad returned from mowing tired and dirty, but a new man. Mom was rested, and content that everything was as it should be. Bunny was just thankful that every one was doing well today. Dad cleaned up for lunch, and they were all able to slip in a nap afterwards. Things were back on track. She could breathe a sigh of relief for now.

Life became less stressful for two full days until the main form of mom's entertainment quit. The TV screen just went blank during one of her afternoon movies. They heard a loud crack, and then the picture disappeared leaving a black screen staring back at them. The picture tube had blown on the ancient set.

"Well, I guess that is that," Bunny's dad stated the obvious.

She disconnected all of the wires, carefully, labeling them so she would be able to set up the DVD player and VCR to another set. Together, they moved the burned out set into the dining room by the garage door to be disposed of later. Bunny was able to cart the small 13" black and white set from the upstairs bedroom to the living room for them to use. After hooking up the cables correctly, they were able to continue with movie time. It wasn't great, but it was better than nothing at all.

"Why is the picture so tiny, and where is the color?" Bunny's mom kept asking. She'd completely forgotten about the entire TV mishap.

They repeatedly told her that the bigger set had blown a picture tube. It didn't register at all. She was beginning to become very agitated. They would have to work on getting another TV very soon.

"First you tell me the washing machine quit. Now you tell me the TV is broken. You guys are just pulling my leg. No body has such bad luck," she told them.

She had remembered the washer incident when they thought she had forgotten all about it, both of them had to laugh in agreement though. They hadn't told her about all the other small things that had gone wrong lately. Like the day the rear view mirror fell off the Jeep's windshield on a trip to town. It nearly scared the life out of Bunny when it crashed to the floor almost causing her to run off the road into a water filled ditch.

Then, one afternoon when she went to the mailbox in the rain to get the mail, and the mailbox door fell off in her hands. She just stood there not quite knowing what to do with it, so it was brought into the house with the mail to hand to dad.

"I said get the mail, not the mailbox." dad told her as he shook his head laughing out loud.

After that there was the evening Bunny plugged in the electric wok to prepare a healthy stir-fry meal. Sparks shot out of the electrical outlet blowing a breaker. The smell of burning plastic filled the room. The incident left her more than a little shaken up. Dad suggested she throw out the devise switching to a skillet on the stove instead. No need to burn the whole house down just yet.

It was unusual for things to constantly break down under normal circumstances, but quite the norm for Bunny's household. They learned to take it in stride rather than fight the inevitable. They would repair, or replace everything some day before JW got home.

Buying a new washer was one thing, but replacing a TV set was quite another. That was JW's department. She knew nothing about the new high-tech sets on the market. Big screen, small screen, flat screen, high-definition, these terms just made her head swim with all the choices. She had no idea where to start, or what JW would want.

It was her dad that came up with a solution. He had to go home to collect mail and check on the house. While he was there, he would bring up an old set they had in storage. It may, or may not work, but it was worth a try. Early the next morning he kissed mom goodbye to set out on his quest to bring it back to Bunny's.

Her mom made note of his absence by constantly asking where he was. It took most of the day for him to complete everything he had to do and get back home. Mom was in a tizzy when he finally arrived late in the afternoon. She immediately reprimanded him for leaving her for days without so much as a goodbye. By the time the other TV was hooked up and running, she had all but forgotten about him being gone at all. Her mood changed as easily as the channels on the set.

Bunny needed Tylenol with a padded cell by the day's end. She went up to bed as soon as her folks turned in for the night after the last round of meds had been handled out. At 2am she woke up vomiting. She spent the next several hours until dawn sick as a dog. Falling asleep on the bathroom floor had given her body more reasons to scream out in agonizing pain. She hoped that it wasn't anything contagious, just a byproduct of stress. The ringing phone at the bedside table brought her back to her soft bed to answer it before it woke up everyone.

"Bunny, it's me, JW. I have had this horrible feeling that something is wrong, so I wanted to talk to you. Are you OK?" JW called to check in before 6am that morning.

"All is well here," she lied through her teeth.

"You sound a little hoarse this morning," he dug deeper.

"Must be allergies. You know how they affect me sometimes," she replied.

They talked for a few more minutes before he had to go. He asked one more time if everything was fine. She stretched the truth to reassure him that all was well and he would be satisfied. She didn't want him to worry about her. He hung up the phone relieved that she had told him her world was simply wonderful. She felt terrible about lying to him, but it was for his own good. It would have only caused him a lot of unneeded stress. Besides, how could he know something was wrong once again?

She slept in as long as she dared, allowing dad to start the morning routine. After she heard mom calling for her, she got dressed to start the day. She would let her dad know about being ill, but kept it from mom. She didn't need her to become upset again. Pepto Bismol and 7-up chasers would be on her menu for the day. She would just take things easy hoping to recover in a few days. Today, dad would have two patients on his hands.

CHAPTER SEVEN

Close to the end of May, Bunny put mom down for her morning nap to run to town. She needed to see an orthopedic doctor about foot pain. She had been having discomfort in her left foot since early March, before JW's had come home on leave. Her regular doctor had checked her over, and taken x-rays, which showed no broken bones. He had thought at first that it could have been a stress fracture. Imagine that, a stress fracture, it just seemed funny at the time to Bunny. When she had told Bea about it she rolled with laughter.

"If stress causes fractures, most of our bones should be broken by now," Bea laughed into the phone.

Medications had not helped much. The outside of her foot was swollen with a large, red bump on the bone just above her little toe. Some days it appeared to be bruised leaving her foot black and blue. Walking was painful, but she had to keep going to take care of everyone. The worst part was that it ached all the time, even waking her at night.

After an exam with more x-rays, she was informed that she had a bunion. Only old people got bunions. She was now officially old. The doctor ordered special inserts for her shoes. He told her to purchase a certain kind of shoe to wear, no more heels or sandals were to be worn, either. She was to return for a check up in a month to see how things were going.

"Bea, I found out what's wrong with the foot. My feet are old. I have a bunion, I also have to wear ugly shoes," Bunny complained. Bea knew how she loved her collection of shoes and array of colorful sandals.

"Welcome to the club. I've got an old, worn out knee. Want to trade a bad foot for a bad knee?" Bea asked her. She had undergone her series of shots for her knee. At the present time she was waiting for relief to arrive any day. It appeared that surgery was in the near future for Bea.

Bunny bought the shoes. She wanted to begin wearing them as soon as she got home that day. The insoles were uncomfortable. It felt like she was walking on sharp sticks. The cure was more painful than the ailment. Not only did the outside of her foot hurt, her arches ached now. Since the insoles were placed in both shoes, both feet hurt, when before only one was affected. She had gone from bad to worse she had twice the pain. She called the nurse two days later to learn that she might have to slowly get used to the inserts. So, she started out wearing them a few hours, then removing them for a few, repeating the process throughout the day. Eventually, she would be able to wear them all day. At some point in time, they would begin to make her feet feel better. If all went well they would realign her bones. When that happened the pain would be gone. Sounded like an easy enough solution to her. She had to keep trying.

It was grass mowing time again all too soon. Dad volunteered to mow if Bunny would keep an eye on mom. Her foot hurt, so she welcomed the help with mowing. She went out to help him get the equipment ready only to find the little trimming tractor with a flat right front tire.

Anticipating problems after the last flat, Bunny had pick up the economy size bottle of "Slime", a product used to repair flat tries without the hassle of removing the tire for a patch. Dad was able to squirt in the required amount of the green goop. The air was added to the tire to achieve the proper level. With all that done, he took it out, and ran it around the yard to coat the inside of the tire. The "Slime" filled any punctures to stop air from leaking out, thus fixing the flat. The mowing could begin as soon as that was done.

According to JW's emails, another band had provided a concert for the troops. It gave them some entertainment, a short reprieve they enjoyed from their daily grind. He also sent along a photo of a large menacing looking, brown lizard that lived in the desert. It was huge about 4 feet in length. The thought of that thing prowling around his area gave Bunny the willies.

He was fine. Things were going as well as could be expected. He was just homesick, requesting more pictures from home. He mentioned that he was feeling a bit under the weather. She hoped he was eating well. Drinking plenty of water was her main concern to stay properly hydrated due to the intense heat.

A package from home was sent quickly with a photo disc of the yard, family, and friends. She added the requested inserts for his boots to cushion his feet from the daily abuse. The rest of the box was filled with little cherry, apple, and blueberry pies. Bunny remembered that one of JW's friends liked cherry pies and licorice, so she had sent him those items in this package as well. Before sealing it up, she placed a 4" rubber chicken toy on the top of the box just for fun. A week later she received a big thanks for the pies. JW loved the pictures of home. The rubber chicken was a big hit. She hadn't realized when she bought it that it was a squeaky toy. It soon became the source of many practical jokes in his unit.

It rained a lot during the last few days of May. In need of time alone, Bunny left dad to care for mom. She needed to check the oil and tire pressure on the tractors. The big old Ford tractor was the most difficult to work on. The tire stems on the back tires were on the inside of the tires, that meant she had to crawl halfway under the thing to even get a reading on the tire pressure.

She had done it before without any mishaps, until today. She lost her balance, slipped, and smacked the bridge of her nose on the tow bar. Pain shot through her whole head as she felt a trickle of warm liquid run down her face. Blood was coming out of her nose, as well as, from the gash on the bridge outside area of her nose. She saw stars for a moment on that one.

Her hands quickly covered her nose as she applied pressure to the pulsating pain while trying to slip into the house unnoticed. Thankfully, both parents were asleep, so she slid past them to the upstairs bath. She washed up, fearfully shooting a look into the mirror, sure enough there was a cut on her nose already starting to swell. It had begun to take on a light bluish hue. She got the bleeding under control. She even tried to apply makeup to conceal the affected area, but it really hurt.

She quickly changed out of the bloody clothes, then went out to lock the shed. Mopping up a few drops of blood off the concrete, she decided to wait until later to attempt that job again. After swallowing up two Tylenol, she was able to finish up her duties inside. Only dad was aware of her accident.

The next morning she woke up to find a swollen, blue nose accompanied by two black eyes. She looked like she'd gotten the worst end of a bad bar fight. A ton of makeup with the help of a small band-aid helped to disguise the wound for now. What a way to start the day.

She decided to tackle the tractors again this morning. When she returned to finish the uncompleted job on the tractors, she found the remaining two tires on the left side of the trimming mower completely flat. She wanted to beat the thing to death with a baseball bat, but her head hurt too much.

"Dad, I found the remaining two tires on the blue tractor flat this morning. You can fix them if you want, or push it out in the yard, and beat it to death. I don't care today," she said as she handed him the bottle of green goop after returning to the kitchen.

"Well, I'm too tired to do that. Since gas is over $3 a gallon, it's too expensive to burn it, so I'll fix it," he said as he took the bottle while hugging his weary daughter.

He finished off the bottle, noting that all 4 tires had been repaired this year. The repairs should hold until JW returned. If they blew again, they'd have to be replaced. They were old and brittle from age; no more could be done for them. The 14year old tractor was held together with a generous length of baling wire, and a prayer the way it was.

After a little over a month with Bunny, the folks were ready to go back to their own home again. Dad spent a couple of days as the head nurse while Bunny stood back to supervise. He was able to keep track of medications, meals, and snacks. Mom's weight was up to 102 pounds. She was stronger, and a little less confused than when she had arrived.

Several times during their stay dad had gotten ill from the chemo tablets he took every evening for his cancer. It wiped him out for a couple of days afterwards. Bunny was worried about him being able to care for himself, let alone mom during these episodes. He had called ahead to enlisted the help of his neighbors in case that happened once they returned home. He promised to call Bunny when it happened, if he needed her help.

Assured that he could handle everything, Bunny cut the apron strings. She was concerned about them, but had to let them return to their home. This time she vowed she would monitor them closer than the last time they ran off on their own.

Emails from JW informed her that temperatures were nearing the 100degree mark. During the winter months it had been in the 80's or 90's during the day, getting very cool, almost downright cold at night. That had come to an end with the heat returning to his part of the world. To make matters worse, during the past month his office had been moved 3 times, each time to a smaller space. People were falling over each other making it increasingly more difficult to work.

Bunny attended the Mustang club annual picnic after church the following Sunday. She would be able to send JW photos of the field of cars lined up on display. Several new members were met, and she was able to visit with dear friends for the afternoon. This outing was needed more than she realized. Her world for the past month or so had been filled with strict schedules and routines. It was relaxing to not be confined to timetables or travel restrictions. There was nowhere she had to be, nothing she had to do. The entire day was spent away from home.

The next morning while cleaning her glasses they snapped in half. The recent blow to her nose may have had a lot to do with the break. She decided that she would go in for an eye exam, and then take it from there. She found a place that would give her a discount with her insurance card. An appointment was set up before investing in new frames, if she needed new lenses, now was the time to get them. She scrounged an old pair of glasses out of her dresser drawer to get by in the meantime. During the exam the doctor told her that her eyes were extremely healthy. Hallelujah for that. She would need new lenses because of an improvement in her eyesight. Frames and lenses were ordered, in week or two she would have new glasses.

Mick's birthday was just four days away, with Father's Day following soon after that. She arranged to have them over for a combined birthday/Father's Day party. He wanted a bratwurst dinner to go with the traditional cake and ice cream. She bought him a circular saw with a laser guide in a plastic case. She knew very little about hand tools, but he mentioned that he needed a saw. Bunny had made a mental note of it. She talked to several clerks, and customers at her favorite hardware store before deciding on one.

"Mom, it's just what I needed. I need some wood to saw," Mick said smiling as he discarded the wrapping paper.

"No scrap of wood in the yard will be safe now," Leann remarked shaking her head.

Bunny emailed JW telling him that for Father's Day she was going to buy him a new, big, flat screen TV. He had jokingly told her several times that he would really like to have one. Since she had no idea what he wanted, she would wait until his return home to let him pick it out himself she told him. That way he would get exactly what he wanted.

He called her on Father's Day, acting all excited about his gift, "Bunny, that is so sweet of you to buy me a big screen TV. I have always wanted one you know. So what have you done now?"

"Can't I just be a generous, loving, wife, buying my dear husband a nice present?" she asked innocently.

"Sure if you want, but what did you break?" he teased, knowing her all too well.

"Well, I just thought you'd like me to spend some money on you since I recently bought myself a new washer. Besides, the TV blew up after the washer went out. I figured we'd both get something out of the deal. I hate to spend all your money on myself," she confessed.

"Oh, Bunny. You, poor thing, I am so sorry. But, do I still get the TV?" he asked.

"Yes, we will pick it out together," she told him.

They talked for a few more minutes. He was relieved to hear that it was old, worn out, items that had bit the dust, not his new tractor, or the new frig.

Dad's 89th birthday was the day after Father's Day. She decided to spend the entire day with him, knowing that everyone else would be there for Father's Day. This would extend the celebration, and he wouldn't be alone on his birthday, since everyone else had to work that day. They took mom out for lunch at a buffet where she ate a good size portion of almost everything in sight. They shopped a little, then spent the afternoon in their living room joking around telling funny stories about each other. Mom was in a cheerful mood, appearing to be on top of things most of the day. She was still gaining weight, which made her look healthier than she had in months. Bunny was pleased that she had decided to delay her trip until today.

A call was placed to talk to the doctor regarding her foot. It hadn't been a month, yet, but she needed to get the appointment moved up. The insoles had helped slightly, but she continued to have problems. Surgery had been discussed at the earlier appointment as an option if the insoles could not provide relief. Knowing this almost threw her into panic mode.

She checked with other people about the doctor that may be cutting on her foot. They all told her he was a very skilled surgeon. She looked at his brochure from the clinic that told her about his qualifications. When she was finished, she felt confident in choosing him for anything that would need to be done.

"Donna, it's Bunny. I need you and John to help me," Bunny called on her mother-in-law.

"You know we will help any way we can. What do you need?" Donna asked.

"My foot isn't getting better, and they moved up my appointment. I need you to go to the doctor's office with me. If he says all that's left is surgery, I need help to decide what to do," she explained.

"What day and time do you need us to go with you?" Donna replied willingly offering their help.

They set up time for a quick lunch with Bunny at her house before setting out to the doctor's office. They had become so close in the past months. Bunny enjoyed their company, depending more on them for guidance. With JW gone, a big decision like foot surgery in the near future she needed help, love, and support from them.

It was the first time that she had to decide on any procedure without the support of her husband by her side. She couldn't ask him what to do about it. He had too much to worry about the way it was. She would not burden him with this. Besides, that whole sermon about rainbows, butterflies, and fluffy bunnies always ran through her mind.

Donna and John were introduced to the doctor. He examined her foot before more x-rays were ordered to see if any changes had occurred. They could try to use injections to ease the pain, but the only real lasting relief would come from surgery. He explained the options of the shots, as well as the surgery, leaving it up to her to choose which course of action she wanted to take. He showed them where the bones need to be straightened, and pieces trimmed away. He explained to them that two small screws would be put into place to hold the bones together. Everything would heal up in alignment ridding her of the pain. The three of them had confidence in the doctor she had chosen. Concerns were addressed. Donna and John agreed with her that the sooner they could get the surgery done, the faster she would begin healing. The shots were only going to delay the surgery, better to meet the problem head on than dance around the issue. It could be done before JW came back to the states. With the matter settled, a surgery date was given for 10 days from then, near the end of June.

She was glad that she had asked them for help. It put her mind at ease knowing that they also thought surgery was the best choice. Next, they set about planning for the day of surgery. They would pick her up to take her in for the surgery. After it was over, Bea would be able to spend a few days caring for her. All of them would keep her secret from JW.

Ten days to prepare for surgery was pushing it, she preferred it this way though. It didn't allow her time to dwell on it, or change her mind. She would be kept busy. The day would arrive before she knew it. Preparations had to be made for the surgery and the recovery period.

Mick showed up early before work one morning to hook up the truck to the trailer for a trash run. He helped her use the end loader on the tractor to load up the burning barrels. He brought discarded items from his place to add to the load, since they were making the trip. They took it in, and unloaded it at the dump, finishing the job by lunchtime. Upon their return, he punched holes in the three new burning barrels that had been delivered earlier that week. After placing them out back, they unhitched the trailer. The truck was put back into the shed. Every thing had fallen into place. What they thought would take two days to finish they had completed in one.

The next day Bunny loaded the bed of the truck full of recycled trash to haul away. She dropped it off, the amount she received from selling the aluminum cans more than paid for the gas. She bought 100 pounds of chicken feed on the way home to top off the storage bin for the hens. A large supply of dog food, cat food, and cat liter was purchased, so there would be enough for a couple of months. She picked up a couple of large bags of dog bones to have on hand as treats for her pup.

She used a power washer to wash down the back of the house and shed. Because of the wet spring with warm temperatures, a green mold had begun to cover portions of house that were constantly in the shade. She had to scrub it with a brush to remove the green, clinging residue. It took most of the day to complete the job. The results were sparkling clean siding, but her foot had her in agony by the time she finished.

John and Donna took her out for lunch before the big day. They ate at a country style restaurant with a covered wagon sitting out front. Donna and Bunny climbed up to sit on the wagon seat. John took photos to send to JW. They were laughing so hard, they almost fell off the thing. The photos would be a preemptive strike to keep him from asking any questions about her health. He always seemed to have this weird way of knowing when something was amiss.

The required pre-surgery check up was preformed with an EKG and blood work one week before surgery, to make sure everything was in order. All the tests came back showing that she was in good health for the operation.

The weather was warm and pleasant. Temperatures were reaching the mid 90's by now. Everyone seemed to be prospering. Jack had six little teeth that could easily be seen when he smiled. His dark brown hair had gotten lighter as he had gotten older. It was turning blonder with every passing day. He was crawling everywhere, getting into all kinds of mischief. Bunny spent as much time with the little guy as she could since she knew she would be out of the picture for some time while healing after surgery.

Two days before surgery, Bunny and Bea shopped for groceries. A supply of healthy frozen dinners, snacks, and salads were purchased to keep on hand for easy meal preparation during her recovery. Thankfully, Bunny hadn't moved the bed back to the guest bedroom upstairs. She would not have to try to maneuver the steps.

Clothes were brought downstairs to be hung in the laundry room for easy access. Toiletry items filled a basket in the bath, so she wouldn't need to go upstairs for anything. The rooms on the upper level would be shut off for now since they wouldn't be in use.

The yard was mowed the day before the surgery. She was ready. JW would have been proud of the way she had handled things in a precise, military manner. She truly was the wife a Soldier.

John and Donna arrived early the next day to take her to the outpatient surgery clinic. Forms were filled out, and copies of insurance cards were made. She was ready for this. A nurse made note of an answer to one question in particular, resulting in Bunny being subjected to a pregnancy test before anything else could be done. She had been too busy to see any pattern, or lack thereof, since JW's leave. After three long, agonizing, minutes, the all clear was sounded. Surgery preparations could continue.

After the IV had been started, the nurse handed her a pen to mark the correct foot for surgery. That was a little unsettling, shouldn't they know these things? Bunny was assured that they knew which foot, but the marking by the patient was added protection. Everyone knew which one, including the patient. She made sure to leave a big black X on the left foot and little toe.

When she was dressed in her surgery gown, Donna and John were allowed in the holding area until time for her to be taken back to the operating room. Bunny quickly related the story about the unscheduled test she had just passed, which filled the room with laughter, then relief. Her in-laws were a blast to have around. She was glad to have them with her during this difficult time, it made things a lot easier. By the time she was taken to a cold operating room, covered with warm blankets and prepped for surgery she was really relaxed.

The doctor arrived as an injection was shot into the IV, she was out. She remembered calling out for JW at some point in the procedure. She heard someone say, "put her back under." It seemed like just a few minutes later that she was awake. Informing her that it was done, a nurse lead her out into the hall to a recliner.

John and Donna appeared to help her with a can of soda, and saltine crackers to snack on. Bunny was beginning to wake up a little. John left to bring the car to the door, as Donna helped her change into her own clothes for the ride home. A stylish, blue, clog looking, boot was adjusted on her bandaged foot. Instructions were given to her for care, and they were off. Everything had gone as planned the doctor told the folks. No problems, nothing out of the ordinary. That was music to Bunny's ears.

They arrived home shortly before Bea popped in. She found Bunny settled in on the couch half asleep with the bandaged foot propped on a pile of pillows. The folks had dropped off a prescription at the local pharmacy, which Bea had picked up for them on her way out.

It was late in the day, almost sunset, before John and Donna left her. After a round of hugs, kisses, and a grateful thank you from her, they headed for home. It had been a long day, but they never left her side. Now, the baton for her care was passed to Bea. She made sure that Bunny was comfortable before asking her what she wanted for supper. She had a taste for pizza, so Bea baked one up for them. After she had food on her stomach, she could have pain medication. It began to act quickly, causing her to drift in and out of sleep the rest of the evening.

Later, she moved into bed with Bea's help. Her foot started to ache, but her good friend filled her full of medication, tucked her in for the night, and went to sleep on the couch nearby. She wanted to be close at hand in case she was needed. A couple of times Bunny got up in the night to move around. Bea was there to assist her getting her back to bed with ice packs on her foot.

Larkin jumped up on her foot once during the night. Bunny howled as Larkin was involuntarily launched off of the bed onto the floor. Bea jumped up thinking Bunny had fallen out of bed. When she got control of herself, she explained to Bea what had happened. They both laughed about the incident, and the startled cat steered clear of Bunny the rest of the night.

The next morning Bea prepared breakfast for them. The day was spent talking, and watching old movies. Bunny was more alert. There was a little less pain than she thought she would have this early in the game. Bea continued her nursing duties all day long. By evening, Bunny told Bea that she was certain she could care for herself. She was up walking able to do simple tasks for herself. It hurt, but it wasn't unbearable pain. She asked Bea to fix her a quick supper, and go home to care for her own family.

Bea made sure all the critters were fed and eggs were collected. She took Goldie out for a walk, so Bunny wouldn't need to worry about that. All she was going to do was eat, then go to bed. Bea left her with a warning to stay inside. She would return to check on her early the next day. Bunny promised to do as instructed, obeying her loyal friend.

For the next five days, Bea continued to come out checking on her, collecting mail, and doing the outside chores. Several times Slick came out with her to take Goldie on long walks to run off her excess energy. Each time he came out the little dog knew he had a special treat for her. She began looking forward to his visits always meeting him with a wagging tail.

After that, Bunny insisted on taking over. She wrapped her booted foot in a plastic bag to protect it from the early morning dew on the grass, and dirt from the chicken coop floor. It was not easy, but she had to get things moving again. Instead of walking out to get the mail she would climb into the car to drive to the mailbox, too much walking caused the pain to return. She knew when to call it quits, her foot let her know when she had to stop. As time went by, she found she was able to attempt a little more time up on her feet.

The 4th of July arrived during her recuperation period. She had many invitations to go out, but she still felt tired, not ready to meet the world full steam ahead. She remained at home to regain her strength, the entire thing had zapped her more than she thought it would.

The Army cooks had prepared a 4th of July cookout for the troops. JW had enjoyed the food and entertainment provided. He even got to spend a little time with his brother that evening, he told her in a short email.

He kept requesting a photo of her. He wanted to be sure she was ok. He just couldn't shake the feeling that something was wrong at home. He knew nothing about the web of lies she had spun the last several months. To appease him Bea and Bunny came up with a plan. Bunny took the boot off her foot to pose for a photo. Goldie sat down in front of her, hiding her one foot when the digital photo was taken. It looked innocent enough. A smiling wife with her faith pup at her feet showing her entire body, except one foot that the dog blocked with her furry body.

After emailing him the photo, he sent a reply that he was content in being able to actually "see" her. She felt bad about the deceit, but if she told him about her problems at home he may become distracted from his business there. That could be dangerous for him. She wouldn't let that happen, his mind had to remain on his duties without distractions from home.

On days when Bunny had been away from her computer, she always called Bea. She would dictate a message for her to send to him, so he wouldn't worry about her. Even if he was out, upon his return he looked for her emails. If his inbox had no messages from her, he would suspect there was trouble at home. So, Bunny and her partner in crime had successfully been able to carry on the charade for months.

Her dad called her two weeks after her surgery to tell her that they were coming up so he could mow the grass for her. It was in need of mowing, but Bunny wasn't going to ask him to do it. She felt terrible every time her 89year old father labored for hours over her yard work. She had decided to let it go until she could tackle it. Besides, he had his hands full caring for mom.

They struck up a deal. If she would entertain mom for the day to give him a rest from his routine, he'd tackle the mowing duties. It was agreed on. Anticipating her condition after surgery she had filled the tractors with fuel. They had been checked for proper tire pressure and fluid levels. The equipment was ready to run. She had even refilled the empty gas cans. In case anyone happened to volunteer to mow, all they had to do was start the equipment to do the job. JW had taught her to always be prepared, and have a backup plan in place in case the first plan fell through. It proved to be a useful tool on more than one occasion.

Mowing the yard was finished in no time at all while she talked with mom. Dad announced that they should all clean up to go out for lunch, just to "blow the stink off" if nothing else. Everyone had been cooped up for weeks in need of a break from the normal activities. Mom ate a hearty lunch, dad looked revived from being able to be out in the fresh air.

Bunny was appreciative of the love her family had shown her yet again. She returned home feeling exhausted, but very blessed. She had a huge weight lifted from her since the yard work was done. She could continue to concentrate on healing.

Two days later she ventured out to church on crutches. She didn't need to use them, but after her first trip out to the diner with her family, she used them for protection. While out that day, she had her foot stepped on by a small child, which brought tears of pain to her eyes. The crutches would keep people a little farther away from the tender foot. She didn't want to repeat an encounter like that any time soon.

The ushers at church put her in the back pew against the wall. A chair was provided to prop her foot up. She joined several others from the church that had recently undergone surgery. They were all recovering from various problems. Walkers, crutches, canes, and pillows lined the floor near their seats. There was a broken foot, a knee replacement, a hip replacement, several sprains, and her foot surgery. She was greeted to their pew with laughter and a round of jokes.

She felt so good after church that she attended the Mustang club meeting. They were preparing for a national show that the club would be hosting this year. She wanted to help if she could. She would not be able to enter her car. She wouldn't be able to get it in tip-top condition alone. That shouldn't keep her from offering her help though, she signed up for an inside sit down assignment.

That Monday she ran into town to have her post-op check up on her foot. The nurse removed the stitches before she was sent off to have x-rays. The doctor appeared shortly after that grinning with delight at her progress. He told her everything looked fine as he popped the films up for her to view.He pointed out the area where the large piece of extra bone had been shaved away. He showed her the screws holding the bones in place. The bump was gone. Bones that had been crooked were now straight. Instructions for continued care were given as he examined the incision site. It was healing nicely.

In four more days she would be able to take a full shower. In 4 weeks she could take off the boot returning to tennis shoes with her special inserts. He wanted to check her again in 4 ½ weeks to make sure things were healing properly. She had gotten through the worst part of the process. Now, she had to let it heal without doing anything stupid like fall or twist her foot. That first shower after two weeks of sponge baths was going to feel great.

Soon she would be ready to get back to her activities that she had missed during the past few weeks. She was still in her boot, but her foot rarely hurt. Just an ache now and then to let her know it was time to rest. A night out to help the car club prepare for the show would be just what she needed to keep her spirits up. She arrived at the home of one of the club members with a batch of brownies. Everyone had brought food for a potluck after the work was done. The whole house smelled wonderful.

She stuffed a few gift bags before deciding to look for another job, one that didn't require standing. She found a place at the raffle ticket table to sit down. She finished up her work for the evening there. Everyone chattered away, the rooms were filled with laughter and fellowship. Once the jobs were done, everyone enjoyed the tables full of food. She was joyfully weary when she returned home late that evening.

CHAPTER EIGHT

She began feeling stronger as the weeks passed. She had enough energy to make her way to the edge of the woods to pick blackberries twice. They were then frozen, so she would be able to bake a pie, or two when JW returned. The early spring frost had taken all of her cherry and apple crop. The berries hadn't bloomed until after the frost. With the spring rains and warmer weather, there was a bumper crop to harvest.

She could feel her body regaining its former vitality, Bunny could finally get out again. It was great to have her mobility back. Bea and Bunny had gone shopping together almost every week since school had let out, and Bea's teaching duties were over until fall. On today's outing Bunny hobbled with her booted foot. Bea limped because the treatments to her knee had failed to produce the desired results. Today's outing was the day to restock Bunny's aquarium with new fish.

"I want something colorful for Jack to watch," Bunny directed Bea to help in her search.

"Hey, come here I found some. One is bright yellow. The other one is a neon blue," an excited Bea called to her.

"They are gorgeous," Bunny said, scanning the tags for their names and price tags.

Bea found them first, "I really have good taste. One cost $22.99, and the other one is only $27.99."

"Listen up, Sparky, if I spend $27.99 on a fish it had better be deep fried served with a big fat steak on the side," Bunny laughed.

They had a lot of fun scanning the tanks for better bargains. They bought ones from a less expensive selection. She ended up buying five fish from the 99cent tank, and two more for $3 each. They were much more in line with her budget.

Bunny emailed the details of their trip to the "fish market" to JW. It amused him that they were having so much fun, and Bunny wasn't sitting at home everyday alone. He was relieved to find out that he didn't own a fish worth $27.99 either.

The following Friday, Mustangs from across the United States, and Canada, began arriving at the hotel parking lot that had been set up for the show. Four of the women from the club tended to the needs of the car owners. They handed out dash plaques and welcome bags. Her shift was from noon to four that afternoon. She loved greeting the owners, and being able to catch a glimpse of their beautiful cars driving by the window. Her shift ended all to quickly for her.

She needed to take in a plate of cookies for the Saturday evening lawn chair social the next afternoon. She ended up volunteering for another turn at the desk, so others could go have supper. Then she joined some friends for a quick bite at a nearby restaurant. Not planning to, she ended up staying for the social hour.

Later in July, Jack was just a few days from turning 11 months old when he let go of the furniture to take his first steps. After he found out that he could move faster using this method of transportation, he took off learning to run shortly after walking. Adding another word to his vocabulary, too. "Uh, Oh" became a popular phrase for falls and dropped toys. All of this information was quickly emailed to grandpa.

The end of July brought cooler weather. It was a welcome change to have mid 80's for highs instead of temperatures that lingered near the high end of 90. The nights were cool and clear. Dad returned to mow Bunny's yard again while the weather remained cooler. He refused to let her on the tractor just yet.

Babysitting on a regular basis for Jack was something Bunny had been missing. She got the chance to watch him the first Saturday in August while Leann held classes for her student. He was dropped off at grandma's place. They started off with a snack, followed by playtime. He was so wired that he refused to stop for his morning nap. Lunch rolled around, and he ate like he was starving to death. After a bottle of formula, he fell asleep in her arms as she rocked him in the same rocker that had lulled his father to sleep years earlier.

A short nap was all it took to recharge him. Forty-five minutes gave him energy enough to continue to play. He sat down at one end of the long hallway as they rolled a ball back and forth for ½ an hour. He was always such a blessing.

Monday Bunny was able to wear both tennis shoes. They felt strange, and her little toe didn't like the tight quarters of the shoe. This was going to take getting used to. Her foot had been held flat for so long that it didn't like to bend, either. At least the fashionable boot was put in the back of the closet out of sight.

An early morning call came in August the 8th from her dad. Bunny thought nothing of the early hour of the call since they all were early risers. But, a few minutes into the call she sensed trouble. He was disoriented and his speech was slurred. All she could get out of him was that he was ill, and he needed help. The phone was handed to mom who tried to tell her what was happening. Bunny informed them that she was on her way down. She threw on the first set of clothes she laid her hands on. Her hair was pulled back, and secured away from her face with a clip. She grabbed her keys and purse before, racing out the door.

Quickly, she dialed the folk's neighbors. Thank God, they hadn't left for parts unknown yet this morning. They answered on the second ring.

"It's Bunny. I need you go over to check on the folks. I got a call this morning, and things just aren't right. I won't be there for an hour and a half, that may be too long," she rushed through the reason for the call.

They quickly agreed to check out the situation. They would call her as soon as they could she was told before the call ended. The Jeep had already covered the entire distance from her home to the highway. She was running as fast as the speed limit would allow and then some.

The phone rang after what seemed to be an eternity. Bunny was informed that a 911 call for help had been made after dad passed out trying to talk to his dear friends. The rescue squad was just pulling up out front, and paramedics were racing into the house.

"Call me when you know where they are going to take him, please. I will continue to head that way," Bunny pressed on giving the Jeep a little more gas, running well over the posted limit.

Nothing was certain, except the fact that dad needed medical attention. Bunny prayed as the Jeep continued to cover the long highway to her destination. Finally, a call came through. Bunny answered knowing it was an update about dad. The paramedics would be transporting him to the nearest hospital to have a doctor evaluate his condition. The neighbors would follow them caring for her mother until she arrived to take over.

The Jeep pulled into the parking lot. Bunny ran past busy construction workers at the ER entrance to find her dad. He looked pale and confused. Mom sat by him crying, just now, aware of the situation.

The story was related to her that dad got up in the middle of the night feeling weak. Mom was trying to get into her medicine bottles for pain pills. He had taken care of her needs, then passed out on the bed. That took place at around 1 am. He had no memory of what went on for the rest of the time between then and the time Bunny had the neighbors check in on her folks. The only thing mom remembered was that he said he felt bad, then he went to sleep. The fact the he had laid on the bed floating in and out of consciousness for at least 6 hours shook Bunny to her very core. What had her mom been up to during that time? Did she sleep, or had she wandered the house in confusion for hours? It terrified her think of what could have take place in that interval.

Dad had been put on oxygen, and an IV had been started before the paramedics left the house. Blood was being drawn for tests as the nursing staff rushed in and out of the room. Confirmation that his hemoglobin level was low indicated some type of internal bleeding. A unit of blood was ordered, arrangements to send him to a larger hospital by ambulance were being made. One of the paramedics on call that day was another neighbor of theirs. She informed Bunny that she would be the one running with the transport to put them at ease. He would have someone he knew with him during the trip. But, since anything could happen on the trip, she had to get him to sign the DNR (do not resuscitate) paperwork, or sign it herself, before transport began. Those were his wishes, thankfully, he was able to put his signature on the paper.

Bunny called her brothers to relay the findings to them. They had been called as soon as Bunny knew that their father was ill earlier in the day. They were already on the road planning to be at the hospital later that day. Since the unit of blood he needed immediately would take an hour to give, Bunny would take mom home to pack clothes. Medications had to be picked up to take with them. Then they would meet him at the other hospital.

It wasn't easy to get mom to pack a bag. She kept walking around the house mumbling to her self, not able to focus on any one task. Bunny racked her brain to remember all the things she might possibly need for at least a couple of days for her care. She stuffed doses of meds and cans of Ensure into a backpack. Clothing was thrown into a suitcase while mom kept trying to hang everything back into a closet, unaware of the need for the packing in the first place. A friend stopped by long enough to distract her. This allowed Bunny to finish the job unhindered. Everything was rushed out, and tossed into the back of the vehicle. Hopefully, she had remembered enough to get by. It would just have to do.

Mom needed to eat something for lunch before leaving. It could be some time before they had the next real meal. Leftovers were warmed in the microwave to serve up. Mom ate everything that was placed before her although she told Bunny that she didn't want to eat not more than five minutes earlier.

A last minute check of the house, a turn of the lock, and they were under way. They made it to the hospital in time to see the ambulance pulling away. Bunny got the floor and room number from them as they passed the ambulance going out of the drive. Now, they wouldn't have to ask a dozen people before they finally found dad. They could go directly to his room.

Bunny tried to get a wheelchair for her mom, but she refused to use it. Instead of wasting time arguing the point, Bunny decided to give into her mother's demand to go without it. The walk turned out to be almost too much for the woman. They had to stop several times to rest before finally reaching his room where they found him in bed as white as the sheets on the bed. They answered questions for the hospital staff most of the afternoon waiting for her brothers to come in. At about 6 that evening they met them in dad's room.

Bunny turned his care over to them, to get mom out for supper, and home to bed. Both were tired beyond words. She had her brothers find a wheelchair for mom while she went to get the Jeep to meet them at the front door.

When she got to the Jeep, she found the rear driver's tire flat, and the front one almost in the same condition. She had run over debris at a bridge construction site on the way to the hospital. Since it was in the middle of her lane of traffic on a two-lane bridge she had no way to avoid it. Her only choice was to go over it, or hit the oncoming vehicles. This brought the count up to 6 flats in about 3 months. She was a little more than discouraged. She had never had a flat in her entire life until recently.

The cell phone was whipped out of her pocket, and a call made to dad's room, "Put everything on hold. I have a couple flat tires I have to figure out how to fix."

"No! You have the worst luck. I'll be right down to fix it. Where are you?" Eugene comforted his little sister.

"I'm in the front parking lot. I'll be the screaming crazy woman running around the parking lot, can't miss me," was all she could say.

She had the little portable air compressor plugged into the car's power port ready for action when he arrived. JW had insisted on keeping it in her vehicle for emergencies.

"What you need is a can of 'Fix a Flat'," her brother added as he inspected the tire for damage.

"Got one in the tool bag. JW keeps me fully stocked," Bunny said handing it to him.

In a few minutes the tires were ready for the road. Dad was where he needed to be. Her brothers would remain with their dad, so she could take care of their mom. After loading her into the Jeep, they headed for Bunny's house. They would face tomorrow's challenges when they came. Right now she had gone through all she could handle. Later in the week she would take the Jeep in to have the tires repaired. They found that the front tire had a 4" nail stuck in it. Her rear tire had picked up a huge 5" bolt, which according to them should have blown the tire right there and then. The tires had carried them over the bridge then on for another 57 miles before going flat. The repairmen had no explanation how they got to their destination before the tires went flat. Bunny knew it was a prayer bringing guardian angels to them that got them there.

CHAPTER NINE

That bed from the guest room still occupied a place in the living room. Bunny had just left it there since it was a pain to keep moving it up and down the stairs. The decision to leave it in place proved to be a prudent one. Not everyone had a bed prominently displayed in the middle of the living room, but it proved to be useful in Bunny's home. After a late supper, medicines were administered, and her mom was put to bed. It took a short time for her to fall into a deep slumber. Bunny slept on the couch a few feet away in case she woke in the night. She did not want her wandering about the house, or worse yet get outside.

The next morning things were clearer in mom's mind. She seemed to understand more about what had happened, and why she had to stay with her daughter. Bunny already had a full day of things to attend to before they went to the hospital, which meant that mom would have to go everywhere with her. Bunny prayed that mom would remain clam. Both would need to have strength for the day ahead of them.

After a phone call to check on her father, she was off to do chores. A quick preparation of a bag of mom's snacks, and they were ready. Bunny had some banking affairs to take care of first. Afterwards, she had her last checkup for her foot surgery before they could go to the hospital.

Mom sat quietly while the banking transactions were done. She accompanied her to the doctor's appointment without any fuss, until x-rays had to be taken. Bunny explained to her that she would be gone for just a little while. An angel of a nurse stepped in to help. She stayed with her, keeping her talking until Bunny returned. Thankfully, the entire office visit took less time than usual. After they grabbed a quick lunch, they headed to the hospital.

The hardest part of the day was getting mom to use a wheelchair once they reached their destination. She was independent, but not strong enough to back it up by walking everywhere now. Bunny hated to order her around, but she had already walked too much today. A repeat of the previous days walk to dad's room would not be repeated today. Besides, they could get to the room faster using this method.

They found dad sitting up in his bed talking, and joking with the nursing staff. It was a relief to see that he had reclaimed his sense of humor. He had received a couple more units of blood, which had brought some color back to his cheeks. He looked better than when they left him, but far from a picture of health.

Every area of his body was x-rayed, scanned, and tested over the next two days. More blood was given to keep his blood count up before they pinpointed the problem. A medication that he had started taking a few months earlier for arthritis pain was the culprit. His doctors were able to stop the bleeding with a minor procedure. The cancer wasn't back as everyone had feared. Their prayers had been heard and answered. Observation for a day or two afterwards would gain his release, if all went well.

The next morning Bunny decided to replace a light fixture in the kitchen ceiling. It shorted out months ago, but the timing hadn't been right to try to replace. She hadn't used it to avoid any problems. All the new parts had been bought waiting for installation. Today was the day to tackle that repair since mom kept turning the on light switch. Bunny had no idea what was happening until she smelled something burning. All she needed was the house to go up in flames. Not knowing how much longer mom would be staying with her, the repair had to be done as soon as possible or risk the chance of being homeless due to a fire.

Unable to contact anyone for assistance on that Saturday, she would give it a go herself. The instructions sounded easy enough. All she had to do was take down the fixture to disconnect the old light, wire up the replacement, and screw in the new fixture. Easy as pie. The first thing she did was shut down power at the main breaker box for the entire house. Maybe that was being too paranoid. But, she didn't want mom to become confused, and by flipping a switch result in her being fried. Better to be safe than sorry.

Sitting in a chair to watch Bunny, her mom became impatient half way through the job. Bunny gave her a flashlight to hold for her while the wiring was completed. It gave her something to do while actually helping a great deal. Both of them had a sense of accomplishment once the light was finally turned on. Since the house failed to burst into flames she considered it a success. Bunny could add electrical engineer to her list of new talents, well, almost.

That afternoon they got a call from Chuck stating that dad was going to be going home later that day. Arrangements were made for them to pick up mom on the way out of town. They would stay on for a while to help out around the folks place. Once dad regained his strength the boys would go home.

Sunday Bunny went to church with a light heart, giving God the glory for His healing and strength. She tried to get back into a routine by attending the Mustang club meeting after church, also. She hadn't heard much from JW; he continued to be in her thoughts. She needed to keep herself busy to stop worrying she told herself.

Eugene called early the next morning to tell her that he would be taking the folks to his place for a short vacation. It would get them away from home. Dad would get as much rest, as he needed to heal after his recent ordeal. That left Bunny free to finish the redecorating she had started on the upstairs bedroom.

Several days she spent painting the ceiling bright white and the walls a steel blue. She placed pale, pink tinted, yellow flowers, and dark, trailing, ivy vines around the wall decorations. Finishing it all off with new floral bedding added the final touch. Light filtering through the ivory sheers gave the room an elegant, but welcome glow. She was glad to have it done after months of delays.

No sooner than she had put away the last of her tools, she got a call about mom. Eugene and Joan had taken her to a doctor to find another infection lurking in her frail body. They sent her back to his house with a bunch of antibiotics to fight it off with instructions to go to the hospital if things got any worse. She was in good hands with Joan as her nurse, but she was in a very frail state. All Bunny could do was to pray, putting everything in God's hands. In the meantime, she tried to keep busy. No word from JW just added concern to her already overactive mind.

She was beginning to drive herself nuts trying to find new projects to work on. She installed a new showerhead in one of the baths. Carpets throughout the entire house were vacuumed and steam cleaned. The lawn was mowed, trimming trees, and shrubs were done. Vehicles were cleaned, washed, and waxed, but still her mind could not find rest. Even attending church service on Sunday couldn't shake the uncertainty she felt.

Checking her emails upon her return from church gave her the answer to the question of why JW had not been heard from for almost a week. She thought he was on a mission since emails sometimes stopped all of a sudden before resuming again. She had become accustom to that part of the separation.

Her heart almost stopped when she opened the account to find no message from JW, but one from his brother. Her hands shook as she uttered a prayer before opening it. JW had been very ill with a case of food poisoning. He had become dehydrated to the point of being admitted to a hospital for IV fluids. His brother had been keeping an eye on him. He was given permission from JW to tell her about it.

She sank in her chair to weep. He was going to be okay; he was sick but going to be fine. A flood of relief poured over her. It wasn't a good thing, but the news could have been much worse. It hurt to know that she couldn't be with him or comfort him. Once again, she turned to God for healing and comfort, this time for JW.

Composing herself enough to send a message back, she thanked her brother-in-law for informing her about JW. Quickly, she sent an email to JW. Knowing that it would be days before he could retrieve it, she had to send it anyway just to let him know that at that moment she was praying for him.

Bad news poured in the following morning like an avalanche tumbling down a mountain. Mom had not responded to the medications. She had been admitted to a hospital several hundred miles away from Bunny, and placed in the Intensive Care unit, her beloved JW was in a hospital half way around the globe, and Dad was still very weak. Bunny was left sitting on the windswept prairie unable to go to any of them.

She could not allow herself to dwell on anything but the positive. Mom would pull through, JW would overcome this food poisoning, and dad would regain his former vitality, it was all in God's hands. All Bunny could do was stay in contact with everyone. She had to keep hope going.

Bea had recently learned that knee replacement surgery was the only way to relieve her pain, every other option had failed. Surgery had been scheduled. Bunny had promised Bea that she would be her coach for therapy afterwards. She proceeded with meetings prior to surgery to find out what her duties would be.

JW was released from the hospital. He would be sent for a period of rest before being placed on light duty. Bunny got several emails downplaying the seriousness of his condition, she had known him long enough to read between the lines, though.

One week after her mother had been admitted to the hospital, her father became ill. He was now admitted to the hospital. Chuck helped Eugene and Joan with hospital duties. With both parents in the hospital, Bunny felt more helpless than ever. The entire situation weighed heavy on her heart. They thought that dad needed to adjust his diet because of a potential gallbladder problem. After two days he was released. But, later that day mom had a mild stroke and massive heart attack. Her lungs were beginning to retain fluids, too. She was slipping. She had received the best of care, but her body was just too weak.

She needed two units of blood to give her strength for upcoming tests. Hoping that they could do something for her, the doctors scheduled tests. They tried, but were unable to open her blocked arteries. Medications would have to be "tweaked" to see if they could get things under control.

An email came in from JW stating that he was ready to resume his duties, and would be gone for about a week. He was well, but leaving to go out. Thankfully, he returned in a little less time than that. Bunny could rest a bit easier once he was back.

Mom's health improved slightly over the next few weeks. After she was released, Eugene brought mom and dad back home on September 8th. Mom was so weak that she was taken directly to a nursing home. She was out of danger for the moment, but needed round the clock care. Dad could visit her daily, if she got strong enough, she could return home soon.

CHAPTER TEN

Bea went in for surgery early one morning in mid September. Bunny sat with Slick the entire day until she could see her dear friend afterwards. The knee replacement had gone well. She was awake and alert when Bunny left her.

Bunny arrived at 7am the next morning ready for therapy duty. Over the next three days, they both learned exercises to stretch and bend the new knee. They had to learn ways of getting in and out of beds, cars, and maneuvering steps. Bea and Bunny had the staff with most of the other patients in stitches from their playful banter.

The ride back to Bea's was very tiring on her, but Bunny made her do a few bends to exercise before she left her. She returned later with dinner for the exhausted family. It felt good to do something instead of waiting for phone calls that seems to bring endless tidings of bad news.

Every morning for the next week, Bunny rose at 5am to finish chores, then to stay with Bea while Slick was working. They had work to do, three times a day they exercised to get her knee working. Bunny was there to push her each day as she coached her through it all. Then, she'd prepare supper for them, slipping off after dishes were done. The next day she would return to torment her friend with more therapy. Bea had cared for her, now it was Bunny's turn to help out Bea.

On the weekends she picked up dad for a visit with mom. Bunny almost gagged at the odor when they entered the doors of the home the first time. A strong smell of disinfectant trying to mask the scent of urine and vomit hit you in the face. The halls were in good condition, but her mother's room was a nightmare.

The floor tile was discolored with age and peeling up around the edges of the room. Plaster was missing from the ceiling. An attempt had been made to replace some drywall near a window, but the job hadn't been touched in years. Her bath had leaky faucets with rust staining the sink and shower. It made Bunny's skin crawl. Dad vowed to remove her as soon as both of them were stronger. Bunny wanted to take them both with her then, but he said he would handle it. And, he did just that a few days later. He showed up, signed her out, and took her home, for which Bunny was very thankful.

After many invitations Bunny had talked Jackie into joining her in church services. She had met her there for many months every Sunday work hadn't called her away. Bunny quickly introduced her to Leann and Mick. The Lord strengthened their bond of friendship through fellowship as they worshipped together. Jackie gave her heart to the Lord early in September, and was baptized shortly afterwards.

While all of this played out, time ticked on, marching toward the end of JW's "boots on the ground" time. He called to tell her to stop sending packages to him in August. He said he had plenty of everything he needed. She would be the first to know when he needed more supplies. She knew by the calendar that she had sent her last parcel overseas to him. Time to come home was drawing near.

Emails stopped soon afterwards. She answered an early call one Friday at 1:30 am to hear his voice, he was in Germany. At 12:30pm the next day he was in New York, back on United States soil, her heart soared. Sure, they had to go through a bunch of paperwork, and out-processing before she had him back, but he was in the states. The information spread quickly that he was on his way home.

In an effort to stay busy and have everything in order, Bunny mowed the yard a few days before he was to come home. In her rush to put away the tractor she stepped off it into a rabbit hole. She landed on her left foot, the surgery foot. Before she knew it she was on the ground in howling agony. The loud pop she heard before the final touchdown in the grass sent pain up her foot and ankle. What had she done?

After lying on the ground letting the pain subside slightly, she rolled up to crawl back onto the tractor. It had to be put into the shed. She hobbled to finish putting away tools. By the time she locked the hens in, it had begun to swell rapidly. Only after everything was done was she free to go inside for a look-see. Once the shoe and sock came off there was no question that she had done something wrong.

The next morning she was sitting in the doctor's office for the results of her "trip down the rabbit hole." Thankfully, no broken bones, just a really nice, painful, sprain. Back to ice packs, and into the blue boot until it healed. That meant that after all her planning, she was still going to meet JW in that blue boot.

Bum foot and all she met JW September 27th at the same Armory where she had left him more than a year earlier. The Central Illinois Mustangers, with others in the surrounding area provided convertibles for the Soldiers to ride in. They met the buses, transferred them into the cars, and the town gave them a welcome home parade. Bunny, JW's younger brother, and her in-laws waited not so patiently for them to arrive at the Armory.

John and Donna were able to meet both their sons outside as the cars unloaded the Soldiers. Bunny wanted to greet him there, but was afraid of having her foot trampled in the stampede for loved ones. Instead, she sat inside the large auditorium waiting. Her Soldier came into the room, and she jumped up to hold him. It was so good to have him back. She never wanted to let go of him again. After several minutes, he asked her why she hadn't met him outside. She looked down pointing to her foot. She had kept it out of the way, hidden until they were reunited.

"What have you done?" he asked, astonished at the wrapped ankle and bulky, blue shoe.

"Better question is, 'what hasn't she done'?" Donna said to him with a wink in Bunny's direction.

Everyone was finally brought into formation and dismissed. He belonged to her again. They picked up a bag of his gear to headed south for home. He was home....he was home.

Bunny's parents were overjoyed that he had returned safely. Her mother wasn't strong enough for the trip to see his homecoming, but he called her when they got home. Knowing he was home thrilled her. JW told her that they would be down in a couple of days for a long visit.

When Leann, Mick, and Jack came to visit shortly after JW's return, he pulled a tattered envelope from his helmet liner. Handing it to Leann he asked, "Remember this?" She opened the envelope and unfolded the letter that included Psalms 91 inside. It was the letter she had given him 15 months earlier.

"It kept me safe. It brought me back home," he told them as he carefully refolded it. "Thank you."

Every morning Bunny had read Psalms 91 out loud as a prayer to protect JW, and the troops involved in the war. Bunny was so thankful. Her deepest desire was to have him back home and safe. And, he had been return to them.

Two days after JW's return, Bunny's happiness began to crumble. A call brought bad news into her world of rejoicing.

"Bunny, it's dad. Your mom is real sick. I'm bringing her up to the hospital," he told her.

"I'll meet you there," she responded, without hesitation, already changing into a clean outfit.

"Baby, I have to go to the hospital. Momma is sick. You rest. I'll be back soon," Bunny explained to JW knowing that he was still feeling the ill affects of all the air travel and climate change.

A long wait in the emergency room would not do anything to help him. And, it was going to be a long wait, she knew from past experiences. He was still trying to adapt to being home. She couldn't drag him out just yet, especially, fearing bad news was on the horizon.

Tests once again confirmed that her heart was at fault. She was admitted to the hospital for tests. JW and Bunny visited her the next day along with Mick, Leann, and Jack. Her mom hugged JW with all her strength.

"You came back. I'm so glad you are alright," she told him while tears rolled down her thin pale cheeks.

"I promised you I would," he replied hugging her gently aware of the fragile frame.

After that she began to slip away. Her heart wasn't strong enough to keep going much longer. Little by little her body began to shut down.

One afternoon during a visit she looked JW in the eye said, "I want to go home. I promised you I'd be here when you came back, but I need to go home now."

JW nodded adding," You hung on and took care of Bunny. Go home…just let go. Go home. I'm here now. I promise you I'll take care of Bunny and dad."

Mick and Leann were with them. They prayed with her, Leann began to pray The Lord's Prayer as mom joined in, which seemed to give her great comfort. A few days later after coming in and out of consciousness, on October 8th she became unresponsive. She went home that morning. She had fought bravely to keep her promise to JW to be there when he returned. He promised her upon his return that he would care for her daughter, and husband of more than 68 years, so she could go home. She left this earthly realm in peace escorted by angels to her heavenly home.

Oh, by the way, everything written here is true. As incredible as it may seem to most people it really did happened, there are witnesses to these events. Some of the names used in this account are fictional. The story, however, is true. It's the account of the life of one Soldier's wife during his deployment, and her attempts to hold it together in his absence. She wasn't a super hero by any means, just an ordinary woman, facing extraordinary circumstances. She was and is a Soldier's wife. Only by the grace of God, and help from his servants on earth was she able to do what she had to do.

Her husband's deployment gave her strength she didn't realize she possessed. It helped her to grow in ways she never thought possible. She found the meaning of family, and the blessings of true friendship. Her heart found a renewed faith in God, giving her the grace she needed to survive. But, that's not the end of her story. She faces adjustments to life after war, so her story continues. Just as the stories and the lives of other families will as they face hardships found during and after war.

Let God pour out his blessings on our Nation. Let God send his peace to the Soldiers, and families who face separation to defend their Country, their Flag, and freedom for all of us. Give them help, hope and love. They are in need of all this and more. God Bless America and God Bless Our Troops!